MAKING MINIATURE DOLLS
WITH POLYMER CLAY

'In small proportions we just beauties see;
And in short measures, life may perfect be.'

BEN JONSON 1572–1637

MAKING MINIATURE DOLLS
WITH POLYMER CLAY

How to create and dress period dolls in $\frac{1}{12}$ scale

Sue Heaser

WARD LOCK

To Jean Lea, my mother, who sowed the seeds of my creativity,
for which I shall always be grateful

First published in the UK 1999 by
Ward Lock
Wellington House
125 Strand
London
WC2R 0BB

A Cassell Imprint

Distributed in the United States by
Sterling Publishing Co., Inc.
387 Park Avenue South
New York NY 10016–8810

British Library Cataloguing in Publication Data
A catalogue record for this book is available from the British Library

ISBN 0-7063-7750-8

Edited by Wendy Hobson
Designed by Isobel Gillan
Photography by Jeremy Thomas
Printed by Dah Hua Printing Press Co. Ltd., Hong Kong

Acknowledgements

I would like to thank the following makers of miniature furniture
for their help with furnishing the room boxes used in the
photographs:

Tudortime Miniatures
Silverweed Cottage
East Coker
Yeovil
South Somerset BA22 9JY
Tudor furniture on pages 66–7, 69 and 77.

Lyntel Miniatures
141 Watling Street
Park Street
St Albans
Hertfordshire AL2 2NN
Upholstered furniture and curtains on page 2; upholstered
furniture on pages 59, 62, 63, 79, 91, 104–5, 111.

David Lee Miniatures
40 Bushwood Road
Kew
Richmond
Surrey TW9 3BQ
Wooden furniture on pages 23, 32, 35, 62, 80, 91, 104.

The room boxes were decorated, and the remaining curtains and
furniture provided, by the author.

Many of the small miniatures used as props in the photographs
are projects from *Making Doll's House Miniatures with Polymer
Clay* by Sue Heaser (0-7063-7590-4, Ward Lock 1997).

CONTENTS

INTRODUCTION

Until relatively recently, the range of materials available for making miniature dolls at home was very limited. Porcelain dolls require expensive kilns, while the air-drying clays are difficult to work to a smooth finish. Wooden peg dolls have great charm but lack realism, and while my mother produced some delightful little pipe-cleaner and woollen dolls for my childhood doll's house, they never looked 'real' either.

All this has changed with the relatively recent advent of polymer clay. As easy to model as children's modelling clays, it needs no specialist equipment and can be baked to a permanent hardness in the home oven. The texture is fine and it has a shelf-life of several years. Once hardened, it is robust and can be carved, sanded, painted, glued and even added to and baked again. Polymer clays are available world wide, they are manufactured in a wide range of colours and most of the major manufacturers produce clays specifically for making dolls.

This book will show you how to make realistic and life-like miniature dolls using polymer clay. The dolls can all be posed and made to stand, sit, bend, kneel or be placed in any other position you fancy! Instructions will take you through every process from sculpting the heads, limbs and bodies to dressing the dolls in a range of costumes from four popular historical periods.

I have given many workshops in recent years on how to make these little dolls and with these step-by-step techniques I have found that anyone can produce results they are proud of. Even if you have never used polymer clay before, you will be using skills developed in childhood of shaping and forming clay. Your first attempts may not be as regular as you would wish but before long you will be delighted with your results. Like any worthwhile craft, practice makes perfect, and after only a little practice, your skills will rapidly improve.

ABOUT THE PROJECTS

The scale of 1:12, often written as $\frac{1}{12}$ (or 1" scale in the US), which is the scale of one inch to one foot, is used throughout this book and this is the most common scale for doll's houses. This means that a 5½ft (168cm) tall woman would be a 5½in (14cm) tall doll. This is a delightful size whether you are making miniature dolls as a hobby in its own right or as inhabitants for a doll's house. Suggestions for working at smaller scales are also given on page 16.

The sculpting instructions make a standard-sized woman, man, child and baby doll and every costume is designed to fit one of these. Each costume is authentic to its period and has been adapted from contemporary sources such as paintings, tapestries, photographs or the actual historical costumes themselves. The periods chosen are some of the most popular with doll's house enthusiasts: Tudor, Regency, Victorian and Edwardian. Within the time band of each period, I have chosen costumes that are relatively easy even for beginners to make in miniature, and which look attractive on tiny dolls.

CHAPTER I

SCULPTING MATERIALS AND EQUIPMENT

This chapter covers all the materials and equipment you will need to sculpt your dolls and all of them are readily available from craft and hobby shops – or you will already have them in your home. Materials and techniques for painting, assembling, dressing and wigging the dolls will be found in their respective chapters.

POLYMER CLAYS

Many different brands of polymer clay are available on the market today and their properties can be summarised as follows:

- They are produced in a wide variety of colours including flesh tones and clays specially designed for doll-making. These colours can be intermixed to produce an even greater range of colour.
- The texture is very fine, allowing detailed modelling in most cases.
- They remain soft until baked and have a shelf-life of several years.
- They are stable while baking; there is negligible shrinkage and virtually no colour change.
- Once hardened by baking at approximately 130°C/275°F in a domestic oven, they can be cut, sawn, added to, re-baked, glued and painted with acrylic paints.
- After hardening they remain slightly flexible and are durable and robust.

Miniature doll-making makes some specific demands on polymer clays and while the many brands available have basic similarities, I have found that they vary considerably when used for small-scale sculpture.

All the projects in this book were made using Fimo's Puppenfimo and this is the clay that I recommend. Many other clays can be used equally successfully but some are less suitable for miniature sculpture and can be discouraging for beginners. The list below gives you this information. If you are a beginner, choose a clay that has good smoothing ability and avoid the softer clays. If you have experience with polymer clay, you will still need to be wary as I have found some clays are virtually impossible to shape into tiny features although they are excellent for larger-scale sculpting.

Softness

The firmer clays are the easiest to use for miniature dolls. They are initially harder to knead but they hold their shape best while sculpting. Clays that are too soft will tend to deform due to the heat of your hands as you try to smooth and sculpt them.

One way to get round this problem with soft clays is to 'leach' the clay. Knead the clay and shape it into a flat pancake. Press this between two sheets of ordinary paper and leave for at least six hours. An oily patch will form on the paper which is the plasticizer leaching out. The clay will now be firmer and far easier to handle.

Smoothing Ability

Polymer clays vary as to how easy it is to smooth the surface of the clay. The ability to smooth in added clay leaving no visible lines is essential for sculpting miniature heads, although it is less important for sculpting limbs and bodies.

Translucency

While a certain amount of translucency is attractive, too much causes miniature features to look almost transparent, while any irregularities in the clay show badly. To overcome this problem with clays that are too translucent, mix in a little white from the same manufacturer's range of clays in the proportion of about 16 parts flesh to one part white. Other colours can also be added to colour the clay.

Strength

Polymer clays vary considerable in strength after baking. The stronger the clay, the less likely the doll will suffer from snapped fingers or broken limbs, especially while it is being dressed.

Quantities

Each doll will need less than 60gm (2oz) of clay, the size of a small pack. The special doll clays are often sold in larger packs of about 500gm (1lb 2oz) and this will be enough for several families of miniature dolls!

THE MAIN BRANDS OF POLYMER CLAY

Polymer clays are widely available from art and craft shops and mail order suppliers. The availability of different brands varies from one country to another.

Fimo

Fimo is manufactured by Eberhard Faber of Germany. Fimo clays are slightly crumbly at first, then knead to a smooth, firm texture. Besides the wide range of colours available, two types are specifically manufactured for doll-making: Puppenfimo and Art Fimo.

1 *Puppenfimo* This is my preferred clay for miniature dolls. It is firm with excellent smoothing ability. The colour is a good opaque flesh tone. The baked clay is of medium strength.

2 *Art Fimo – Doll Pink* Another doll clay produced by Fimo, this is not as widely available as Puppenfimo and must be baked at a maximum temperature of 100°C/212°F. Firm, good smoothing and with a pleasing, slightly translucent colour, it has a lower strength after baking.

3 *Fimo – Flesh Colour 43* This is part of the widely available range of coloured Fimo. It is firm with good smoothing ability and a slight translucence. It has a medium strength after baking. As it is sold in small 60g (2oz) packets, it is a useful beginners' clay.

Formello or Modello

Manufactured in Germany by Rudolf Reiser, this is known as Formello in the UK but Modello in some countries. The flesh clay is opaque but rather bright and looks best when mixed with white and/or translucent clay. It is firm, has good smoothing ability but lower strength after baking.

Polyform Products

This US company produces several different clays: Super Sculpey, Premo Sculpey and Sculpey III.

4 *Super Sculpey* This clay is a beige flesh colour. A soft clay, it is improved by leaching (see page 7). As it is quite translucent, I prefer to add a little white. It has good smoothing qualities but lower strength after baking.

5 *Premo Sculpey* This clay has replaced the original 'Promat' clay and comes in a large range of colours. The flesh clay (called beige) is quite soft and translucent so it is improved by leaching and adding white (see pages 7 and 8). It has good smoothing qualities and is strong after baking.

A mixture of equal parts Super Sculpey and Premo Sculpey flesh improves the qualities of both clays and is recommended by the manufacturer.

Sculpey III This clay has a large colour range which includes flesh but as it is a very soft clay, I cannot recommend it for my miniature dolls as it does not hold its shape while sculpting in miniature.

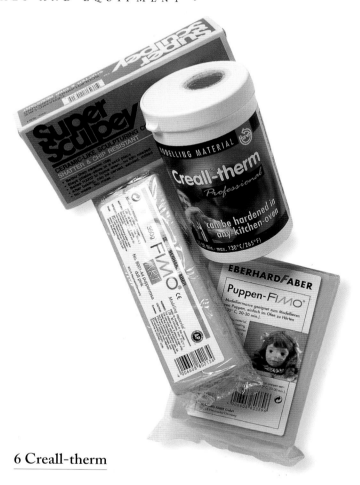

6 Creall-therm

Manufactured in Holland by Havo BV, the flesh clay is slightly translucent with a beige flesh tone. Leaching improves the clay for miniature techniques (see page 7) and the smoothing ability is good. The baked clay is strong and has a pleasant texture. Bake at 150°C/300°F.

Du-kit

Manufactured by Creative Products in New Zealand, the flesh clay is opaque but rather tan coloured, although this can be adjusted by mixing in other colours from the range. It is firm with good smoothing and extremely strong after baking. Bake at 150°C/300°F; it may crack or 'sweat' if baked at too high a temperature.

Cernit

Cernit is made by T + F GmbH in Germany and includes special doll clays in a variety of colours. It has long been a favourite with doll-makers because of its flesh-like appearance and is used to make extremely life-like dolls by many talented artists. However, it has little smoothing ability so I cannot recommend it for my miniature dolls. It is strong and flexible after baking.

Modelene

The Australian polymer clay, this comes in two qualities: regular Modelene and Artists' Modelene, the latter available in a good range of flesh colours. While it is used to produce beautiful larger dolls, it has little smoothing ability so I cannot recommend it for my miniature dolls. It is very strong after baking.

MIXING THE BRANDS

Because the various brands of clay have such different qualities for sculpting and making dolls, there has been a great temptation for doll-makers to mix brands in order to find the perfect clay for their personal needs. However, there have recently been reports that mixing doll clays from different brands may affect long-term durability. If you want to mix, it is advisable to stick to one manufacturer's clays as these should be compatible.

STORING CLAY

Store your clay in a cool, dark place to lengthen its shelf-life and to prevent it going hard and crumbly. Opened packets are best stored in an airtight tin and will then keep for several years. Avoid plastic containers as they may be damaged by being in contact with polymer clays.

OTHER MATERIALS

Mix Quick

Mix Quick is made by Fimo. It is a softening agent for mixing with clay if you find it too hard.

Methylated Spirits (Denatured Alcohol)

Used to clean your tools and the board you work on, methylated spirits are also useful for degreasing the baked clay before painting and for washing brushes after using spirit-based varnish. Nail varnish remover is an alternative.

Wet Wipes

You will need to clean your hands frequently while working with flesh-coloured clays to prevent dirt on your hands from marking the pale clay and wet wipes are very effective.

Talcum Powder

Useful for dusting over the clay to prevent it becoming sticky, talcum powder can also be used as a release in push moulds so that the clay does not stick to the mould.

Glue

The white glue in stick form that is available from stationers for gluing paper and card is used to smear on to baked clay to make fresh clay adhere more easily.

Superglue can be used to repair any breakages of baked polymer clay.

BASIC EQUIPMENT

Most of the basic equipment needed for making polymer clay miniature dolls can be found in your home. The following list gives all the tools used for the projects in this book.

- A board or surface to work on. A smooth melamine chopping board is ideal, or else a Formica table mat or a ceramic tile. A thick sheet of glass with the edges sanded smooth and placed over graph paper will give you instant measurements as well as an ideal surface. Some of the sculpting methods use the natural tack of the clay in order to press clay on to the work surface where it will stick lightly while you work on it. Be sure that your surface is smooth enough to do this.
- A craft knife (X-Acto knife) with a rounded blade as shown in the photograph. This shape of blade is the most versatile and can be blunted slightly before use by running it over a steel as razor-sharpness is not necessary and may damage your board.

- A ruler to check the size of balls and other shapes.
- A baking tray lined with non-stick baking parchment.
- Fine 400 and 600 sandpaper to smooth baked pieces.
- A piece of quilt wadding (batting) or stiff fabric to restore the patina to sanded areas.

SCULPTING TOOLS

You will need a collection of miniature sculpting tools and most of these can be found in your home.

Blunt-ended Wool or Tapestry Needles

These are my main sculpting tools at this scale. The stainless steel has a wonderful smooth surface that will leave no marks on the clay as you smooth and sculpt. Keep several sizes handy. You will also need a needle or knitting needle about 2mm ($^3/_{32}$in) thick to pierce holes in the doll bodies and limbs. This size gives a hole that is just the right size to take the pipe cleaners used for jointing the dolls.

Darning Needle

This is used for nostrils and other details and for piercing holes through the body and limbs of the baby dolls. It should make a hole big enough to take 0.6mm jewellery wire.

Pencil

Use the side of a smooth, round pencil to make a shallow indent when shaping faces.

Glass Ball-headed Pins

The glass head is invaluable for smoothing and shaping round the eye sockets. To stop any unexpected pricks, make a handle for the pin by embedding most of the shaft in a log of polymer clay and baking it.

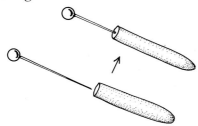

Measuring Card

You will constantly need to measure the diameter of clay balls and the thickness of logs. In order to do this accurately, make a card template. Along the edge of a piece of stiff card, mark off sections in the following sizes, leaving about 10mm ($^3/_8$in) between each. You may need two cards to cover all the sizes:

2mm ($^3/_{32}$in)	10mm ($^3/_8$in)
3mm ($^1/_8$in)	13mm ($^1/_2$in)
4mm ($^5/_{32}$in)	15mm ($^5/_8$in)
5mm ($^3/_{16}$in)	18mm ($^{11}/_{16}$in)
6mm ($^1/_4$in)	20mm ($^3/_4$in)
7mm ($^9/_{32}$in)	23mm ($^7/_8$in)
8mm ($^5/_{16}$in)	25mm (1in)

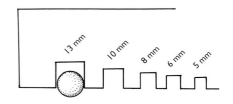

Cut out the sections, making each one deeper than it is wide. When you form a ball or a log, it is simple to hold the template over the clay to measure the diameter or thickness. You can estimate smaller measurements using the 2mm ($^3/_{32}$in) section.

Instep-former

This is a useful tool that you can make out of polymer clay to help you to sculpt heeled footwear for your dolls. Roll a 6mm ($^1/_4$in) thick log about 25mm (1in) long. Slope one side all along its length as shown in the illustrations and flatten the top. Bake for 10 minutes.

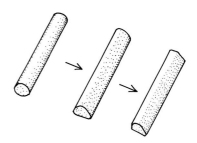

Paintbrush

Use a small, soft paintbrush to brush over the clay when you have finished sculpting. This helps to remove fingerprints and small imperfections.

Purchased Tools

These are by no means necessary, but if you enjoy sculpting you may find you want to purchase a few. Stainless steel dental tools and miniature sculpting tools in smooth hardwood or stainless steel are the best. You can often find these in sculpting and hobby catalogues.

CHAPTER 2

SCULPTING TECHNIQUES

Be sure to read through this chapter before you begin to work as many techniques referred to in the projects are only covered here so as to avoid constant repetition. Techniques for painting, assembling, dressing and wigging the dolls will be found in their respective chapters.

MIXING CLAY COLOURS

Polymer clays come in a wide range of colours that can be combined to make further colours. This means that you can create a palette of clay in the same way as an artist mixes paint. To mix, work the different-coloured clays together until all streakiness has disappeared.

The projects in this book use the basic flesh tone supplied by the manufacturer and for miniature dolls with white skin, I find this is perfectly adequate as you can add subtle changes with washes of acrylic paint after baking if you wish. As you become more advanced, you may want to vary the flesh colour by mixing in coloured clays for dolls of different ages or ethnic groups and it is fun to experiment. The flesh-coloured clays of the different brands vary quite a lot and preference is usually a matter of personal taste. Only mix clays from the same manufacturer (see page 10).

Coloured clays are used to make polymer clay miniature buttons (see page 58) and you can mix the colours to match the fabric.

SCULPTING

You do not need any previous experience to start sculpting the dolls using the step-by-step instructions in this book. The illustrations and templates are there to help you and all you need to do is to work methodically through the instructions. Take care to work as close to the measurements given as possible as this will help to keep your work to scale and will ensure that the clothes patterns fit when you come to dress your dolls.

Before starting, read through these notes so that you are familiar with the basic techniques. Then, if you are a beginner, start with the instructions for a woman doll as these are the most detailed. If you find that your first attempt is going wrong, set it aside and start again with a fresh piece of clay. The unbaked clay is infinitely reusable as long as you keep it clean, so nothing will be wasted. The more you sculpt, the better you will become and the more delighted you will be with your results!

Preparing to Work

Before starting, wash your hands and wipe down your board with wet wipes or methylated spirits to ensure everything is as clean as possible. The flesh-coloured polymer clays are particularly prone to picking up dirt, apparently from nowhere, while you work so you will need to be extremely careful to keep your work surface and hands clean at all times.

Kneading the Clay

All polymer clays must be kneaded thoroughly before use and this is best achieved by repeatedly rolling and folding the clay. This is not just to make it soft and malleable, it will also eliminate irregularities in the clay, remove air bubbles and make the clay stronger after baking. If the clay feels very hard when you first begin to work it, warm it in your hands or on a hot water bottle.

Sometimes the clay seems to remain crumbly and hard despite thorough kneading, which usually means that it is old stock. Try mixing it with Mix Quick mixing agent (made by Fimo) or kneading in a little baby oil or vegetable oil. Clay that becomes too soft in your hands to hold its shape can be rested in the refrigerator for a while to cool, or it can be leached (see page 7). A dusting of talcum powder helps to prevent the clay sticking.

SCULPTING BASICS

The instructions for making the various parts of the dolls all start with either a clay ball or log of a specific size. The measurement given for a ball is always the diameter, while that of a log is the thickness and the length needed. You should find that you can make balls and logs instinctively but here are a few tips to help you to make them really even.

Making Balls

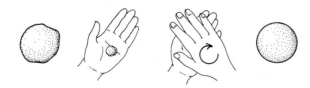

Shape a ball roughly the right size and rotate it between your palms, using a heavier pressure first, then a lighter pressure as the ball takes shape.

Measure the ball with your card template or ruler, then adjust the size by pinching off or adding clay as necessary and rolling again.

Making Cylinders or 'Logs'

Making cylindrical shapes is an important part of working with clay. Practise rolling the clay into even logs of different thickness. Start with a ball of clay and roll it between your hands to make an oval.

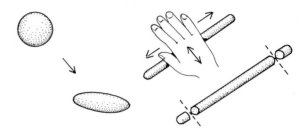

Place this on your working surface and roll it smoothly back and forth with your hand, always keeping your hand moving up and down the length of the log and not pressing too hard. You can then trim the ends and cut accurate lengths as required.

Working with the Knife

The craft knife with a curved blade is an invaluable tool. It is not only useful for cutting the clay to the required sizes but also as a delicate applying tool when your hands would soon distort the clay.

Tiny slices of clay are best applied by scooping up each one on the tip of the knife. It should cling to

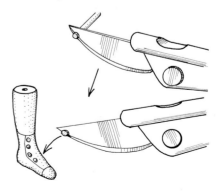

the blade sufficiently for you to turn the knife over to place it and then you can use the blade to press it lightly down. This technique is used to apply slices of clay for ears, and buttons and straps to footwear.

Applying and Smoothing Clay

You will often need to add more clay as you sculpt, such as to add a nose or to accentuate the chin or plump the cheeks. Form a piece of clay of the size required and press it gently on to the clay surface, being careful to position it accurately. Now use a sideways smoothing action with the side of a wool needle or modelling tool to smear the edges of the applied piece outwards into the surrounding clay.

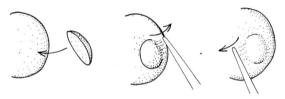

You should be able to remove all signs that the piece has been added. Use a fingertip to stroke the clay smoother and then a gentle brushing with a soft paintbrush will complete the final smoothing and remove any fingerprints.

Sculpting the Head

This is the part of the body that takes longest to sculpt, and if you have warm hands you may find the clay becoming too soft. To avoid this, push a knitting needle or skewer into the clay where the neck will be and use this to hold it while you are working.

BAKING

Place the finished pieces on to a baking sheet that has been lined with baking parchment. Most polymer clays should be baked in the oven for about 20 to 30 minutes at 130°C/275°F (approximately gas mark 1) but check the packet instructions first. All the project instructions give suggested baking times.

It is advisable to measure your oven's temperature carefully with a separate oven thermometer to ensure that the temperature is correct. Oven thermostats can vary quite widely and if the clay is baked at too high a temperature, it will discolour, while toxic fumes can be given off if it burns. If the temperature is too low, the clay will take a long time to harden or may remain fragile, and applied pieces will drop off easily. Be particularly careful in checking gas ovens as there is a considerable temperature range from the top to the bottom of the oven.

The clay will not harden until completely cool but it can be replaced in the oven and baked again if you are not satisfied with the hardness. There may be a slight discoloration of pale colours after prolonged baking.

SAFETY

Polymer modelling clays are all made from fine PVC particles suspended in plasticizers that give the clay its malleability and softness. Baking the clay causes the PVC particles to fuse together into a permanent plastic which is a stable product but there may be traces of plasticizer left that can continue to leach out. All the proprietary clays are labelled non-toxic but, as with any art and craft medium, it is sensible to follow some basic precautions.

- NEVER allow the clays to overheat, as when they burn they produce toxic fumes. If you accidentally let the clay overheat, turn off the oven at once and ventilate the room thoroughly. Avoid breathing any fumes.
- Always wash your hands after using polymer clays.
- Do not allow polymer clays to come into contact with foodstuffs, even after baking.
- Do not use the same utensils for polymer clays and food.
- Supervise young children when handling the clays.

FINISHING TECHNIQUES

Sanding and Carving

The robust nature of polymer clay means that it can be sanded after baking and this is very useful if you find you have fingerprints or other irregularities on the surface. Sanding can also be used to reshape areas. The best types of sandpaper to use are the finer grades, 400 and 600. Once sanded, the clay will show a lighter surface covered in small scratches. To remove this and restore the original patina, rub the clay surface firmly with a piece of quilt wadding (batting) or stiff fabric.

The baked clay can also be carved with a craft knife to adjust the shape of features or limbs or to shape the ends of limbs for jointing. Take care when cutting, and support the piece well so it does not snap under the pressure of the blade. It is difficult to carve the clay to a smooth finish so you will need to sand the carved areas.

Adding to Baked Clay

This is useful to round the back of a flat head, to build up heels on shoes or to rebuild or repair any area after carving. Roughen the surface with sandpaper, smear with some stick glue and apply fresh clay. The glue will help the fresh clay to adhere to the baked clay. Smooth in the edges with a tool and your fingers, then sculpt as required. Bake the piece, then when it is cool, sand gently to smooth the joins if necessary.

Repairing Breakages

Small breaks can occasionally occur if the doll is roughly handled, and fingers and wrists are the most vulnerable. Glue the broken piece back in place with Superglue, which will make a very strong bond. Any rough edges can then be sanded smooth or holes filled with fresh clay and the piece re-baked.

SMALLER SCALES

The instructions given for making the dolls also work very well at the smaller scale of 1:24. You will need to reduce the templates to 50 per cent on a photocopy machine, then follow the instructions halving all the measurements given. Use jewellery wire in the same way as for the baby dolls to assemble the adult and child dolls, and use fine beading wire for baby dolls.

The costume patterns can be reduced in the same way but you will need to adapt the sewing techniques considerably for such tiny clothes.

MAKING MOULDS

The head is the part of the doll that takes the most time to make and for this reason it is often useful to make a mould from a head you have sculpted so that you can then reproduce that head as often as you wish. Not only can you make a duplicate of your original but you can alter the moulded head to create a new head, avoiding all the preliminary sculpting.

I use white polymer clay to make moulds from my sculpted heads and the results are excellent owing to the fine texture of the clay. It is preferable to use white clay to avoid any possible staining of the flesh colour by darker clays. These simple one-part moulds are often called push moulds.

Making a Push Mould from a Sculpted and Baked Head

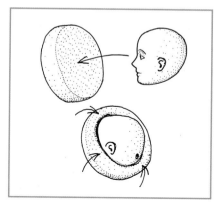

1 Form a ball of well-kneaded white clay about the size of the head you are going to mould. Flatten the ball into a disc about 50mm (2in) across and smear the surface with talcum powder. Press the head to be moulded into the centre of the disc, face first, positioning the nose in the centre.

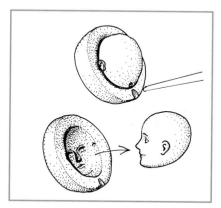

2 Carefully draw up the edges of the clay disc around the sides of the face until they are level with the ears all round. Mark the position of the bottom of the head on the mould. Ease the head out of the mould, taking care not to distort it. Bake the mould for 20–30 minutes.

Making a Moulded Head from a Push Mould

1 Dust the mould with a paintbrush dipped in talcum powder, brushing out any excess which would otherwise spoil the surface of the moulded head. Form a ball of clay the same size as the original head. Cut about one-third off the back of the head. Shape the front of the head into a point for the nose and press this into the mould, making sure that the point goes into the nose cavity of the mould.

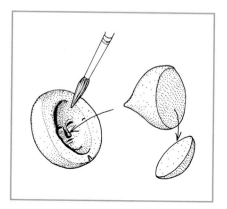

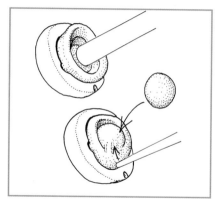

2 Using the end of your craft knife or the handle of a wooden spoon, ram the clay hard into the mould. You will need to push quite hard to be sure that the clay is forced down to the end of the nose cavity. This will make a hole in the centre back while the sides rise up. Shape the cut-off third into a ball and press this into the hole, smoothing the sides over it to make the back of the head as rounded as possible and sloping into the back of the neck.

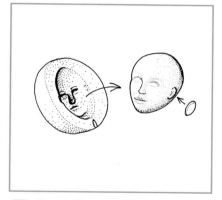

3 Carefully ease the head out of the mould. If you are not happy with the result, try again. You will need to make a neck hole and add ears as the moulded ears will probably be too indistinct. You can then sculpt the head further if you wish.

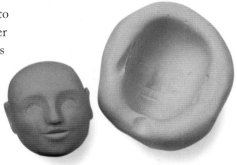

CHAPTER 3

SCULPTING THE DOLLS

This chapter shows you how to sculpt all the basic parts of each type of doll. Follow each step carefully, paying close attention to the measurements given. The actual-size templates give you the proportions to follow, while the measurements in the text will keep you to scale. For each doll, sculpting the face and hands is the most challenging part and you will need to practise these. People often find that their first attempts at sculpture look older than they would wish but do not be disheartened as this is quite normal! Make a few trial heads to start with and you will find that your sculpting improves rapidly and you will soon achieve faces to be proud of.

Besides using the illustrations and photographs in this book, refer frequently to photographs of people from catalogues or magazines to give yourself inspiration. Observation is another important tool. Study the faces of family and friends for expressions and features to incorporate into your tiny dolls.

The sculpting instructions also show how to sculpt lower legs complete with the various boots and shoes that are appropriate for the different costumes. While it is possible to make shoes from kid leather and fabric, polymer clay is an ideal medium for simulating leather and the resulting footwear can be made to look very realistic. It is also possible to sculpt lower legs in the colour of the stockings so that only the shoe colour needs to be painted. However, coloured clays are not always as easy to sculpt with so I prefer to use flesh clay.

PREPARING TO SCULPT A DOLL

The tools and materials you will need are the same for each project in this chapter and are described in Chapter 1.

All the holes to be made through the limbs and body of the adult and child dolls should be large enough to take a pipe cleaner snuggly. Use a 2mm ($^3/_{32}$in) thick wool needle to make the holes (see page 11). The baby doll is assembled using 0.6mm jewellery wire and therefore needs narrower holes made with a darning needle (see page 12).

USING THE TEMPLATES

You will frequently need to measure your sculpting against the doll templates. To avoid staining the pages of your book with clay, trace the templates in ink on to tracing paper. Do not use pencil or it will leave marks on the soft clay. You can then keep the template beside your work as you follow the steps to sculpt and assemble a doll.

Detailed instructions for assembling and painting as well as posing the dolls are given in Chapters 4 and 5.

Sculpting a Woman Doll

*These instructions are for a woman of average height,
approximately 168cm (5ft 6in) at a 1:12 scale. The features need
to be regular and well smoothed for a young woman.*

WOMAN DOLL TEMPLATE
Actual size template and assembly
diagram of the woman doll.

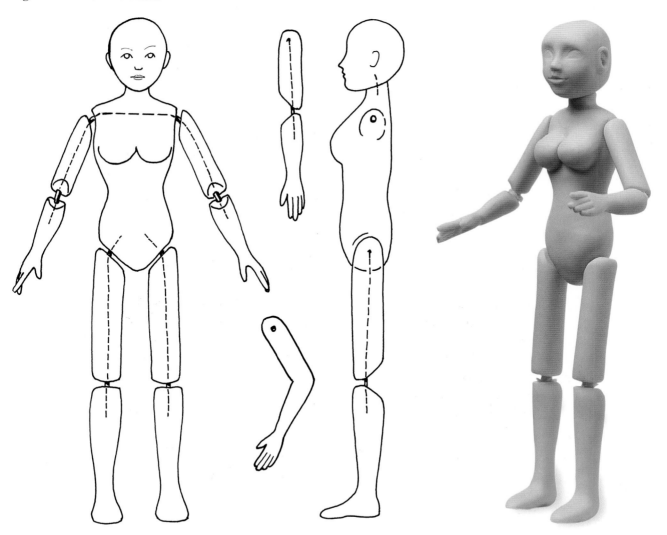

THE HEAD

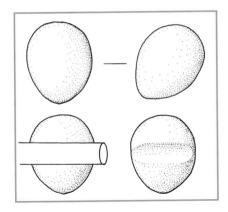

1 Form an 18mm ($^{11}/_{16}$in) ball of clay. Roll the bottom lightly between your hands to form an egg shape with the pointed end for the chin. Hold it at the angle shown in the drawing at the top right – this is the side view and shows how the chin needs to be positioned so that it is tipping upwards. Turn the head to face you and press the side of a pencil into the clay about half way up the front to make a shallow impression across the face. This is the position of the eye sockets.

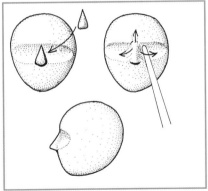

2 Form a 3mm ($^{1}/_{8}$in) ball and shape into a teardrop for the nose. Press this into the indentation as shown, point upwards, and smooth in the sides and top with the side of the blunt needle (see page 15). Check the profile and smooth the clay into the shape shown. You can tip the nose up slightly or keep it straight, depending on the effect you want.

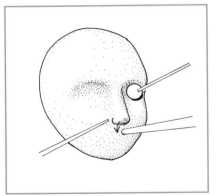

3 Use the ball-headed pin tool to make impressions for the eye sockets, keeping them as even as possible. Thin the nose by stroking downwards with the tool. Smooth the joint between the nose and the top lip. Accentuate the line round the sides of the base of the nose. Smooth away any hard edges on the cheeks and brow.

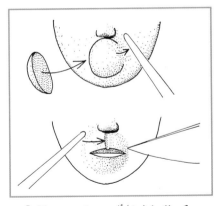

4 Form a 3mm ($^{1}/_{8}$in) ball of clay, flatten it into a pad and apply it to the mouth area of the face, smoothing the joins. This gives you a dome of clay on which to sculpt the mouth. Make a cut with the knife along the line of the mouth about 3mm ($^{1}/_{8}$in) below the bottom of the nose and about 5mm ($^{3}/_{16}$in) long. Use the blade of the knife to open the mouth a little. Make a slight indentation in the centre of the top lip as shown, running down to the mouth.

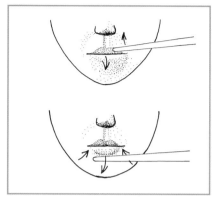

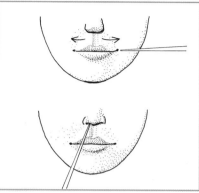

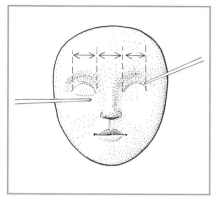

5 Smooth the upper edge of the mouth cut by stroking upwards with the side of the needle. Repeat for the bottom edge by stroking downwards. Make a horizontal impression about 1.5mm ($\frac{1}{16}$in) below the mouth cut to emphasize a bottom lip, smoothing down to the chin and upwards on either side; the bottom lip should be slightly narrower than the top lip.

6 Use the point of the needle to emphasize the mouth: a tiny hole at each corner of the mouth will give a slightly amused look, while faint downwards lines from the corners will make the face more severe. Smooth outwards on either side above the mouth if it is too prominent. Pierce two nostrils with a fine needle. This will cause the base of the nose to flair out slightly. Do not overdo this!

7 Using the tip of the wool needle, draw in the upper eyelid line and make another line just above it. Very lightly suggest the bottom eye line by pressing the side of the needle along the line as shown. The eyes each need to be about 3mm ($\frac{1}{8}$in) wide with the distance of one eye between them. Compare your doll's profile with the drawings.

8 At this point you can add a flattened ball of clay to emphasize a weak chin and pinch it into a pretty shape, smoothing the joins. If the back of the head looks too flat, it is best to add a little more clay after first baking the head, otherwise it is easy to spoil the face. Cut two thin slices from a 5mm ($\frac{3}{16}$in) log for the ears and apply in the position shown. Each ear needs to be in the centre of the head when viewed from the side and positioned between the brow bone and the bottom of the nose.

THE ARMS

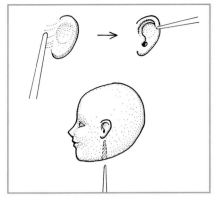

9 Indent the centre of each ear with the ball tool and smooth in the side towards the face. Mark a curve just inside the outer edge and then draw an 'S' curve inside it, reversing this for the other ear. Make an ear hole as shown lower down at the base of the 'S'. Make a hole with the 2mm ($^3/_{32}$in) wool needle centrally underneath the head where the neck will go. Brush over the face with a soft paintbrush as a final smoothing.

10 Bake the head for 20 minutes. When it is cool, you can add extra clay if necessary to build up the back of the head into a good rounded shape (see page 16 for tips on adding clay).

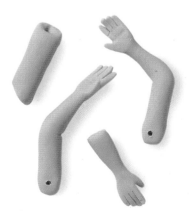

1 **Upper arms** Form a 6mm ($^1/_4$in) log of clay and cut two 23mm ($^7/_8$in) lengths. Pierce each one right through with the wool needle, pushing the clay back into shape if it distorts. Pinch the shoulder into a rounded shape and angle it on the side that will be towards the body. Angle the bottom of the upper arm for the inside of the elbow. Twist the needle to free it and remove it from the clay.

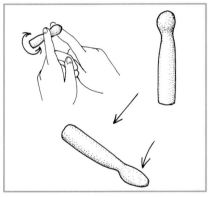

2 **Forearms** Each forearm and hand is made all in one. Form a 6mm ($^1/_4$in) log and cut two lengths each 30mm ($1^1/_4$in) long. Round one end of each and thin 10mm ($^3/_8$in) from the end for the wrist by rolling between your forefingers. Press the resulting ball end on to the board to flatten it to about 3mm ($^1/_8$in) thick, thinning it towards the end. The hand area should now be held by its own tackiness to the board.

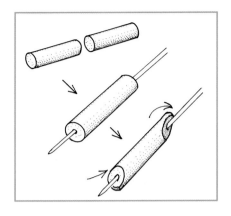

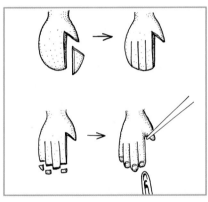

3 **Hands** Flatten the other hand next to the first so you can work on both together to keep them symmetrical. Remember to reverse the fingers for the second hand! Cut away a V section with your knife to make a mitten shape. Cut a line in the centre of the finger area, then make a cut on either side of this to create evenly spaced fingers. Trim the fingers as shown. Use the blade of your knife and your tiny tools to round each fingertip and smooth the edge of the V cut. Mark nails using the eye of the large wool needle.

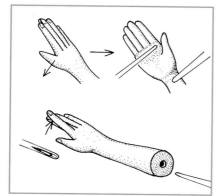

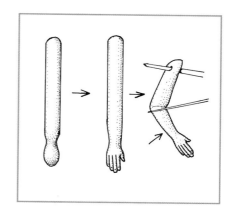

ALTERNATIVE ARMS FOR SHORT SLEEVES

The Regency costume has short sleeves and this needs arms that are made all in one.

Cut two 40mm (1½in) lengths from a 6mm (¼in) log. Make a hand at one end of each as in Steps 2 to 4 above. Check the length against the template and trim if necessary. Shape the tops of the shoulders as before and pierce each shoulder right through with the wool needle. Hold the fine needle against the inside of the arm at the elbow and press the lower arm upwards to make the elbow crease and bend the arm. Arrange the arm into a natural angle.

4 **Finishing the hands** Slice under each hand with your knife to remove it from the board and push the thumb downwards. Mark the fingers on the underside. Mark lines along the base of the fingers and on the palm with the wool needle, using your own hand as a guide. Accentuate the wrist with the side of a round tool. If you wish, separate the forefinger by cutting through the clay and pushing the finger up slightly. Arrange the hand into a natural pose and mark a thumbnail.

5 **Arm length** Check the length of the forearm against the template and trim if necessary. Make a hole in the end of the forearm about 6mm (¼in) deep with the wool needle.

THE LEGS

1 **Thighs** Roll out a log 8mm (⁵⁄₁₆in) thick and cut two 35mm (1³⁄₈in) lengths. Pierce both with the needle as for the upper arms and pinch the tops of the thighs to angle the side towards the body. Shape the backs of the knees at an angle. Remove the needle and refine the shaping, taking care not to distort the holes.

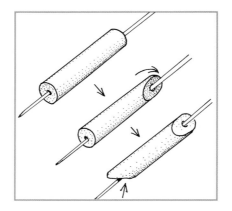

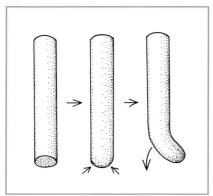

2 **Lower legs** The shoes or boots will be painted in the appropriate colours after baking. For all styles, form a log 8mm (⁵⁄₁₆in) thick. Cut two pieces 40mm (1½in) long and round one end of each length. Pull down the heel at a point 13mm (½in) from the end to make a hockey-stick shape. Pulling the heel down rather than bending the foot up prevents the clay creasing at the ankle.

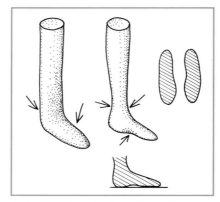

3 **Shaping the legs** Press the foot down on to the board, flattening the toe end and shaping the heel. Model into a foot, straighter on the inside and curved on the outside. Indent the inside of the instep slightly. Thin the ankle by rolling it between your two forefingers, and model the leg so that the shin is straight and the calf swells at the back. If the doll is to have shoes rather than boots, shape the ankle thinner. Now follow the instructions for the required footwear.

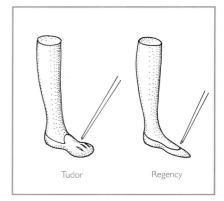

Tudor   Regency

4 **Tudor shoes** Shape the toe fairly wide and draw in the line of the upper with the point of the wool needle. Mark a few slashes on the toe.

Regency slippers Shape the foot into a slightly pointed, slim shape. Mark on the details of the shoe upper with the wool needle.

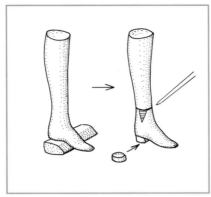

5 **Victorian boots** Form each foot into the shape of an ankle boot with slightly square toes. Press each boot down on to the instep-former (see page 12), flattening the sole of the foot on to the board and the heel on to the former. This will curve the foot into a raised heel shape. Cut two small heels about 3mm (1/8in) long from a 5mm (3/16in) log. Press one on to each heel and press the foot down on to the board so that the foot rests flat. Use a needle to mark on the boot upper with 'elastic inserts' in both sides.

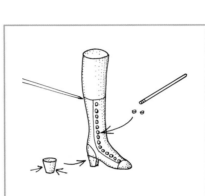

6 **Edwardian boots** Follow instructions for the Victorian boots using the instep-former but make the heels higher and pinch them in at the bottom as shown. Draw on a top line above mid-calf and mark a line down the outside of each boot. Cut tiny slices from a 1.5mm (1/16in) log for the buttons and apply with your knife all down the sides (see page 14).

7 **Finishing the feet** Measure the leg against the template and trim to length. Make a hole about 6mm (1/4in) deep in the top as shown. The back of the knee will be cut at an angle after baking to avoid distorting the modelled foot. Be sure that the leg is completely upright when the foot is flat on the board or your doll will not stand firmly.

8 **Baking the limbs** Bake all the limb pieces for 25 minutes.

THE BODY

1 **Shaping the body** Form a 25mm (1in) ball of clay. Shape into an oval and press on to the board so it is about 13mm ($^1/_2$in) thick. Work into shape using the template as a guide, nipping in the waist, flattening the top, and shaping the body into a point at the bottom. Apply two 8mm ($^5/_{16}$in) balls to the chest front. Smooth these in at the top to make the bust.

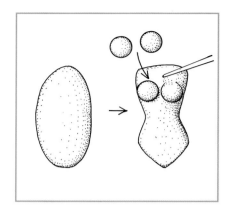

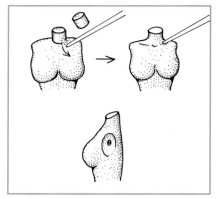

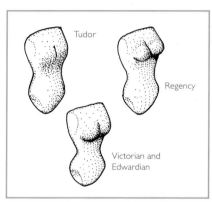

2 **Period details** The shape of the body needs adjusting according to the period of the doll. The Tudor bust should be flattened as though it is contained in a flat-fronted corset. The Regency bust needs to be fairly high and pushed upwards with an attractive cleavage. The Victorian and Edwardian busts should be lower than the Regency one and fairly full. Take care to model the body accurately to the template as this will mean the costumes will fit easily. For all periods, indent the small of the back slightly.

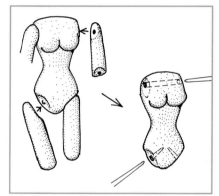

3 **Arm and leg holes** Take the baked upper arms and press them hard into the clay at the shoulders to shape the clay to the arm tops. Do the same with the thigh pieces. Pierce right through the upper body at shoulder level with the wool needle, using the imprint from the upper arms as a guide to the position of the holes. Repeat for the leg holes but make two leg holes, piercing upwards 6mm ($^1/_4$in) deep into the body.

4 **The neck** Cut a 5mm ($^3/_{16}$in) slice from a 5mm ($^3/_{16}$in) log and press on to the body. Smooth the join into the shoulders. Suggest collar bones as shown if the doll is to wear a low-necked dress.

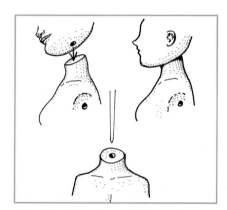

5 **Shaping the neck** Press the baked head on to the neck, trimming the neck to fit at the angle shown. Make a hole in the neck where the head hole has left an impression. Take care that the body arm hole remains open.

6 **Baking** Bake the body for 20 minutes.

Assembly Instructions for assembly are on page 46.

Sculpting a Man Doll

Men dolls are made using same basic techniques as for women dolls but the details are different in virtually every way. Faces are more angular and stronger featured, hands and feet are larger, bodies are a completely different shape and limbs are longer and less curving. The man doll is approximately 15cm (5⅞in) tall or the equivalent at 1:12 scale of 180cm (5ft 10in).

MAN DOLL TEMPLATE
Actual size template and assembly diagram of the man doll.

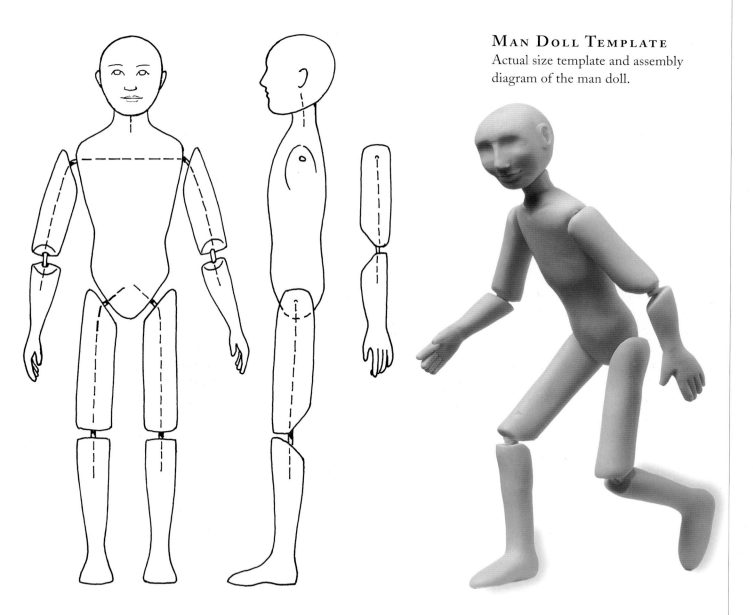

THE HEAD

1 Form a 20mm (³⁄₄in) ball of clay. Shape it into an egg shape as shown in the diagram. The chin needs to be stronger and more angular than for the woman doll. Hold it at an angle as shown in the drawing at the top right. Turn the head to face you and press the side of a pencil into the clay about half way up the front to make a shallow impression across the face. This is the position of the eye sockets.

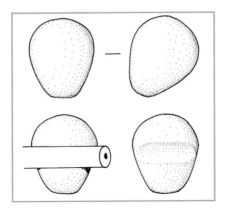

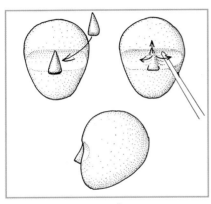

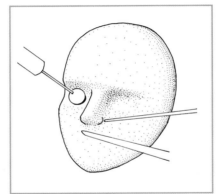

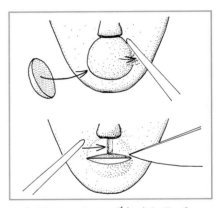

2 Form a 4mm (⁵⁄₃₂in) ball and shape into a teardrop for the nose. Press this into the indentation as shown, point upwards, and smooth in the edges with the side of the blunt needle, keeping the sides fairly upright and the nose angular. Check the profile; a notch under the brow bone will give a more masculine appearance but do not overdo it!

3 Use the ball-headed pin tool to make impressions for the eye sockets, keeping them as even as possible and the top of the socket fairly straight. Thin the nose by stroking downwards on either side with the tool. Smooth the joint between the nose and the top lip. Accentuate the line round the sides of the base of the nose.

4 Form a 3mm (¹⁄₈in) ball of clay, flatten it into a pad and apply it to the mouth area of the face, smoothing the joins. This gives you a dome of clay on which to sculpt the mouth. Make a cut with the knife along the line of the mouth about 3mm (¹⁄₈in) below the bottom of the nose. Make this 5mm (³⁄₁₆in) across, or wider for more character. Use the blade of the knife to open the mouth a little. Make a slight indentation in the centre of the top lip as shown, running down to the mouth.

5 Smooth the upper edge of the mouth cut by stroking upwards with the side of the needle. Repeat for the bottom edge by stroking downwards. Make a horizontal impression about 1.5mm (¹/₁₆in) below the mouth cut to emphasize a bottom lip, and smooth upwards on either side. Keep the lips fairly thin and define the corners of the mouth.

6 Pierce two nostrils with the wool needle which will cause the base of the nose to flair out slightly. Using the tip of the wool needle, draw in the upper eyelid line and make another line just above it. Very lightly suggest the bottom eye line by pressing the side of the needle along the line as shown. Make the eye shape slightly angular and allow one eye width between the eyes.

7 Flatten a 3mm (¹/₈in) ball of clay and apply to the chin, smoothing in the joins. Check the profile and adjust as necessary. You will find you can press the chin into more prominence and accentuate the brow bone as you wish – the clay should allow a fair amount of movement. Try pinching the face thinner, making the cheeks more angular and marking a cleft in the chin. Cut two thin slices from a 5mm (³/₁₆in) log for the ears and apply in the position shown.

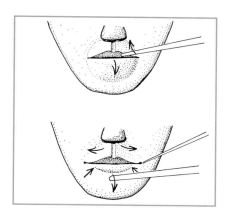
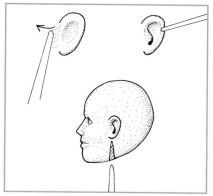
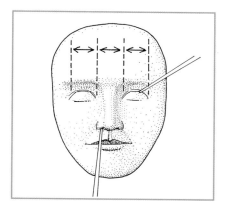
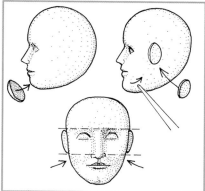

8 Smooth in the side of each ear towards the face and indent the centre with the ball tool. Mark a curve just inside the outer edge and then draw an 'S' curve inside it, reversing this for the other ear. Make an ear hole lower down at the base of the 'S'. Make a 6mm (¹/₄in) deep hole with the 2mm (³/₃₂in) wool needle centrally underneath the head where the neck will go. Brush the face with a soft paintbrush as a final smoothing.

9 Bake the head for 20 minutes. When it is cool, you can add extra clay if necessary to build up the back of the head into a good rounded shape (see page 16 for tips on adding to baked clay). This is particularly important for a man doll that will have short hair. Bake the head again for 20 minutes.

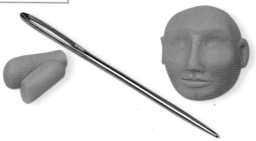

THE ARMS

1 **Upper arms** Form an 8mm ($^5/_{16}$in) log of clay and cut two pieces 25mm (1in) long. Pierce these all through their length with the wool needle and roll them back to shape on your board if they distort. Pinch the shoulder into a rounded shape and angle the side that will be towards the body. Angle the bottom for the inside of the elbow. Twist the needle to free it and remove it from the clay.

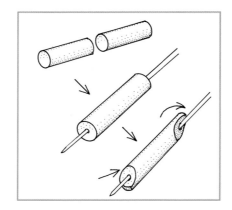

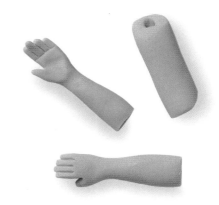

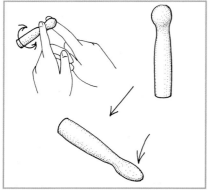

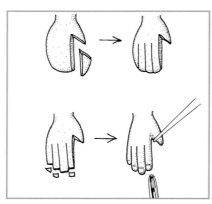

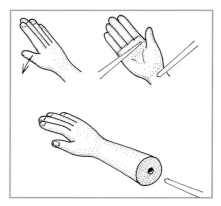

2 **Forearms** Each forearm and hand is made all in one. Form a 7mm ($^9/_{32}$in) log and cut two 30mm (1$^1/_4$in) lengths. Round one end of each and thin about 10mm ($^3/_8$in) from the end for the wrist by rolling between your forefingers. Press the resulting ball on to the board to flatten it to about 3mm ($^1/_8$in) thick, thinning it towards the end. The hand area should now be held by its own tackiness to the board.

3 **Hands** Flatten the other hand next to the first so you can work on both together to keep them symmetrical, reversing the shaping for the second hand. Cut away a V section with your knife to make a mitten shape. Cut a line with your knife in the centre of the finger area, then make a cut on either side of this to make evenly spaced fingers. Trim as shown so that the central finger is the longest. Round each fingertip and mark nails using the eye of the large wool needle.

4 **Finishing the hands** Slice under each hand to remove it from the board and push the thumb downwards. Mark fingers on the underside, curving the hand round into a natural shape – you can cut between the fingers to separate them if you wish. Mark lines along the base of the fingers and on the palm. Accentuate the wrist and mark a thumbnail. Check the length of the forearm against the template and trim if necessary. Make a hole in the end of the forearm about 6mm ($^1/_4$in) deep with the wool needle.

THE LEGS

1 **Thighs** Roll out a log 10mm (³⁄₈in) thick and cut two lengths of 40mm (1¹⁄₂in). Pierce both with the needle as for the upper arms and angle the tops of the thighs towards the body. Shape the backs of the knees at an angle. Remove the needle and refine the shaping, taking care not to distort the holes.

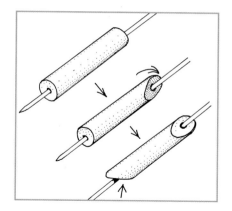

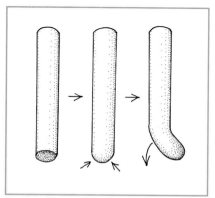

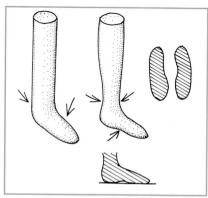

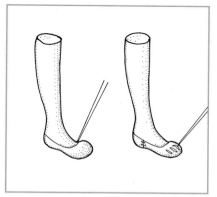

2 **Lower legs** The shoes or boots will be painted in the appropriate colours after baking. For all styles, form a log 10mm (³⁄₈in) thick. Cut two pieces 50mm (2in) long. Round one end of each length. Pull down the heel at a point 15mm (⁵⁄₈in) from the end to make a hockey-stick shape.

3 **Shaping the legs** Press the foot down on to the board, flattening the toe end and shaping the heel. Model into a foot, straighter on the inside and curved on the outside. Thin the ankle by rolling it between your forefingers, and model the leg so that the shin is straight and the calf swells at the back. If the doll is to have shoes rather than boots, shape the ankle thinner. Now follow the instructions for the required footwear.

4 **Tudor shoes** These are flat and wide at the toe and can be quite exaggerated. Shape the toe fairly wide and draw in the line of the upper with the point of the wool needle. Leave the shoe plain or mark slashing lines and stitching details if you wish.

5 **Regency shoes** Shape a slim shoe and use the instep-former (see page 12) to make a raised heel by pressing each foot down on to the instep-former as shown. Cut a 1.5mm ($\frac{1}{16}$in) slice from a 5mm ($\frac{3}{16}$in) log, trim the front, and apply to the bottom of the foot for the heel. Press the foot down on to the board to ensure the foot rests flat. Mark on the line of the shoe upper. Using your knife (see page 14), apply two small rolled-out rectangles of clay for tongues. Cut strips of clay to suggest buckles and apply to the front of each shoe as shown.

6 **Victorian boots** Men wore ankle boots with a low heel similar to women. Make the foot slim with a square toe and apply a low heel as for the Regency shoes, using the instep-former to shape the foot. Use a needle to mark elastic inserts on each side of the upper of each boot.

Edwardian shoes Shape the foot into a shoe with a pointed toe and high upper. Apply a low heel as for the Regency shoes. Mark on the upper details and laces.

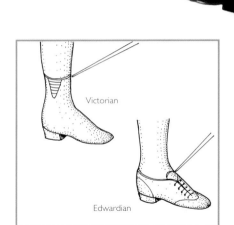

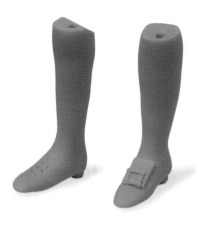

7 **Finishing the feet** Measure the leg against the template and trim to length. Make a hole about 6mm ($\frac{1}{4}$in) deep in the top as shown. Make sure that the leg stands firmly and fully upright or the doll will not stand properly. The angle behind the knee will be cut after baking to avoid distorting the soft leg.

8 **Baking** Bake the limb pieces for 25 minutes.

THE BODY

1 **Shaping the body** Form a 30mm (1¼in) ball of clay. Shape into an oval and press on to the board so it is 15mm (⅝in) thick. Shape as shown with the widest point at the shoulders and the bottom of the body forming a point, using the template as a guide. Press on the baked upper arms and thighs in position and shape the clay to fit.

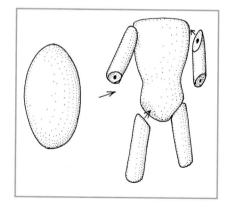

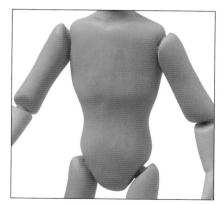

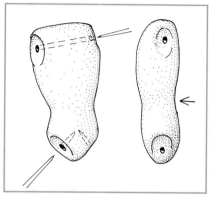

2 **Arm and leg holes** Pierce right through the upper body with the wool needle for arm holes, using the impressions from the upper arms as a guide to the position of the hole. Make two leg holes, piercing upwards 6mm (¼in) deep into the body and using the impressions as a guide. Check the side view and indent the back slightly.

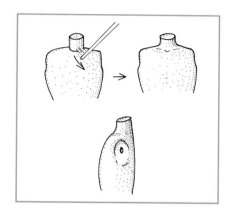

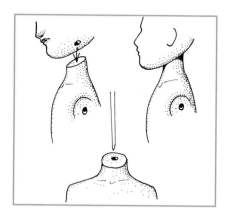

3 **The neck** Cut an 8mm (⁵⁄₁₆in) slice from an 8mm (⁵⁄₁₆in) thick log for the neck and press on to the top of the body. Smooth the join into the shoulders with the side of the wool needle. Check that the side view matches the diagram. Make a slight indentation at the top centre front of the chest and suggest collar bones as shown if the doll is to wear an open neck.

4 **Shaping the neck** Press the baked head on to the neck, trimming the top of the neck to fit the underside of the head. The head needs to be at the angle shown to look natural. Make a hole in the neck where the hole in the head has left an impression. Take care that the body arm hole remains open.

5 **Baking** Bake the body for 20 minutes.

Assembly Instructions for assembly are on page 46.

Sculpting Older Dolls

*Ageing the sculpted face can sometimes happen without you intending it
because sculpting older dolls is often easier than sculpting young and beautiful ones!
Observe older faces carefully for the many different ways that flesh wrinkles
and apply these observations to your sculpting.*

BASIC INSTRUCTIONS

If you wish to sculpt an older man or woman doll, start with the basic instructions given for their younger counterparts and then apply the following alterations. Use discretion depending on the intended age of the doll. The side of a fine needle is a good tool for making wrinkles.

THE FACE AND NECK

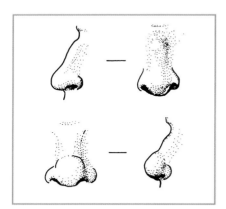

1 **Nose** You can make the nose larger and full of character. For men in particular, make the nostrils large and gently flare out the base of the nose.

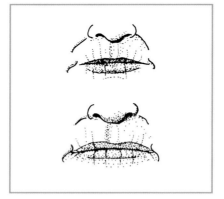

2 **Mouth** Make the lips fairly thin and mark tiny lines across them. Accentuate the smile lines running down from the nose. Lines running down from the corner of the mouth make a bad-tempered face so use these with care.

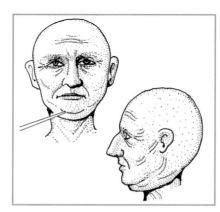

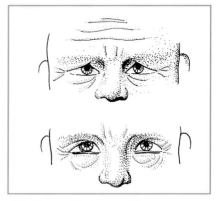

3 **Brow** Horizontal lines across the brow are typical as are small lines above the nose.

Eyes Mark crow's-feet and lines under the eyes. Do not make the eyes too large. Older eyes are often more triangular in shape as shown.

4 **Chin** Suggest a double chin by marking a small chin above the bottom of the face. Add extra clay under the chin if the doll is intended to be fat.

Neck Press lines at the angle shown into the clay.

Face sides Mark a few wrinkles in front of the ears and down the sides of the face to suggest sagging flesh.

THE HANDS AND BODY

Hands These are a part of the body that should show age as much as the face. Mark lines along the back of the hands and across the backs of the wrists. Older men's hands can be made larger and full of character.

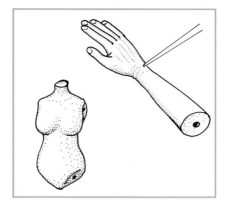

Body For women, you can make this fatter with less of a narrowing at the waist and with a fuller and lower bust. Men's figures can be the same as a younger man or you can add a round belly for stoutness. In all cases, remember to compensate in the clothing patterns for the fuller figures by cutting the side seams wider for bodices and waists. You can also stuff a little quilt wadding or cotton wool inside the clothes to plump out a figure.

Sculpting Child Dolls

These instructions are for making child dolls 10cm (4in) tall which is the 1:12 equivalent of an eight-year-old. Younger or older children can be made quite simply by shortening or lengthening the arms and legs a little; the head and body remain virtually the same. There is very little sculptural difference in the faces and bodies of young boys and girls at this scale so these instructions serve for both.

THE HEAD

1 Form a 15mm (⅝in) ball of clay. Shape it into a fairly round egg shape and hold it at an angle as shown in the top right side view. Turn the head to face you and press the side of a pencil into the clay about half way up the front to make a shallow impression across the face. This is the position of the eye sockets.

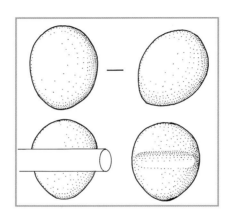

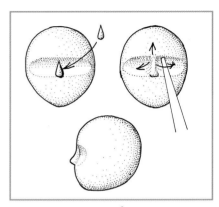

2 Form a 2mm (³⁄₃₂in) ball into a teardrop. Press this into the indentation as shown, point upwards, and smooth in the edges with the side of the needle. Check the profile and smooth the nose into a gentle curve. The nose needs to be small with a low bridge and the cheeks left full and chubby.

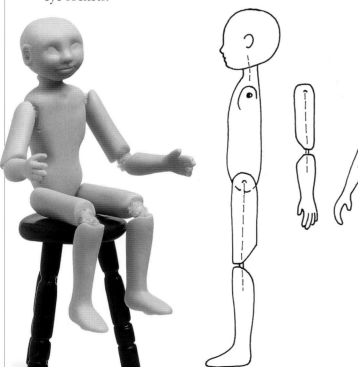

CHILD DOLL TEMPLATE
Actual size template and assembly diagram of the child doll.

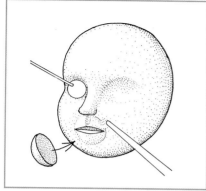

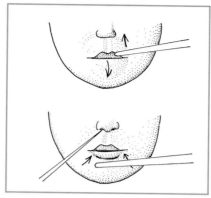

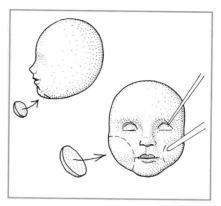

3 Make gentle impressions for the eye sockets with the ball-headed pin tool, keeping them as even as possible. Apply a flattened 3mm ($\frac{1}{8}$in) ball of clay to the mouth area and smooth in the edges. Make a cut 2mm ($\frac{3}{32}$in) below the bottom of the nose along the line of the mouth and use the knife blade to open the mouth a little. Make a slight indentation in the centre of the top lip as shown, running down to the mouth.

4 Smooth the upper edge of the mouth cut by stroking upwards with the side of the needle. Repeat for the bottom edge by stroking downwards. Make a horizontal impression about 1.5mm ($\frac{1}{16}$in) below the mouth cut to emphasize a bottom lip, smoothing down to the chin and upwards on either side. The top lip should be slightly wider than the bottom. Keep the mouth small and full-lipped. Mark nostrils with a fine needle point.

5 Check the profile and add a flattened ball to the chin if necessary, smoothing in the edges. You can point the chin slightly to make the face more elfin. Add flattened balls to the cheeks as well if they do not look full enough. Smooth in all the joins and brush with a paintbrush. Avoid any hard angles in a child's face. Draw in the upper eyelid curve and make another line just above it, allowing one eye width between the eyes. Lightly suggest the bottom eye line.

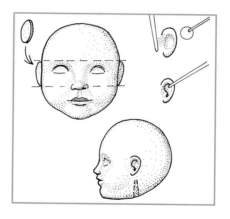

6 Cut two thin slices from a 4mm ($\frac{5}{32}$in) log for the ears and apply to the sides of the head, aligned as shown. Smooth in the sides towards the face and indent the centres with the ball tool. Draw an 'S'-shaped curve on each ear and make an ear hole at the base of the 'S'. Make a 6mm ($\frac{1}{4}$in) deep hole with the 2mm ($\frac{3}{32}$in) wool needle centrally underneath the head where the neck will go.

7 Bake the head for 20 minutes.

THE ARMS

1 **Upper arms** Form a 5mm ($^3/_{16}$in) log of clay and cut two pieces 20mm ($^3/_4$in) long. Pierce these all through their length with the wool needle. Pinch the shoulder into a rounded shape and angle it on the side towards the body. Angle the bottom of the upper arm for the inside of the elbow. Twist the needle to free it and remove from the clay.

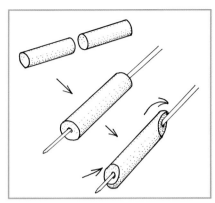

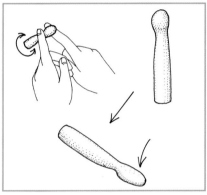

2 **Forearms** Each forearm and hand is made all in one. Form a 5mm ($^3/_{16}$in) log and cut two lengths each 15mm ($^5/_8$in) long. Round one end of each and thin the log 7mm ($^9/_{32}$in) from the end for the wrist by rolling the log between your forefingers. Press the ball on to the board to flatten it to about 2mm ($^3/_{32}$in), thinning it towards the end. The hand area should now be held by its own tackiness to the board.

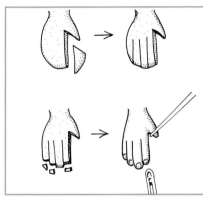

3 **Hands** Flatten the other hand next to the first so you can work on both together to keep them symmetrical, reversing the fingers on the second hand. Cut away a V section with your knife to make a mitten shape. Cut a line with your knife in the centre of the finger area, then make a cut on either side of this to make evenly spaced fingers. Trim the fingers as shown. Round each fingertip and mark nails using the eye of your large wool needle.

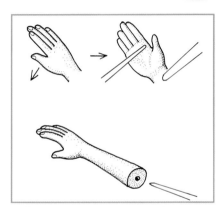

4 **Finishing the hands** Slice each hand off the board and push the thumb downwards. Mark fingers on the underside, curving the hand round into a natural shape; you can separate the fingers by cutting between them if you wish. Mark lines along the base of the fingers and on the palm. Accentuate the wrist and mark a thumbnail. Check the length of the forearm against the template and trim if necessary. Make a hole in the end of the forearm as shown about 5mm ($^3/_{16}$in) deep with the wool needle.

THE LEGS

1. **Thighs** Roll out a 6mm (¼in) log and cut two lengths of 23mm (⅞in). Pierce both with the needle as for the upper arms and angle the inside top of each thigh by pinching it to shape. Shape the backs of the knees at an angle. Remove the needle and refine the shaping, taking care not to distort the holes.

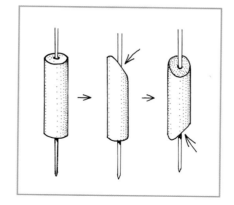

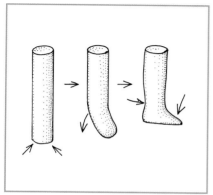

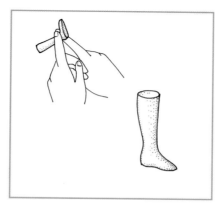

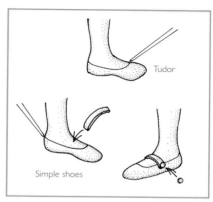

2. **Lower legs** The shoes or boots will be painted in the appropriate colours after baking. For all styles, form a log 6mm (¼in) thick and cut two pieces 30mm (1¼in) long. Round one end of each length. Pull down the heel at a point 10mm (⅜in) from the rounded end into a hockey-stick shape. Press the foot down on to the board, flattening the toe end and shaping the heel. Model into a foot, straighter on the inside and curved on the outside.

3. **Shaping the legs** Thin the ankle by rolling it between your forefingers and model the leg so that the shin is straight and the calf swells at the back. If the doll is to have shoes rather than boots, shape the ankle thinner. Now follow the instructions for the required footwear.

4. **Tudor shoes** Shape the toe fairly wide and draw in the line of the upper with the point of the wool needle.

Simple shoes These are suitable for many costume periods. Shape the foot into a slim, slightly pointed shape. Mark on the details of the shoe upper with the needle. For shoes with ankle straps, cut a thin strip of clay and use your knife to apply it over the instep as shown (see page 14). Gently press on a tiny ball of clay for a button on the outside of the strap.

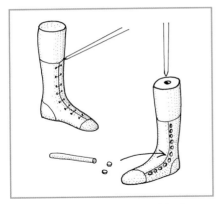

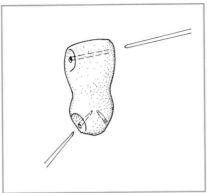

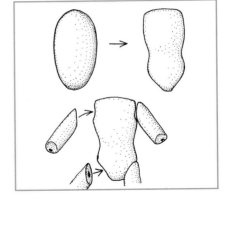

THE BODY

1 **Shaping the body** Form an 18mm ($^{11}/_{16}$in) ball of clay. Shape into an oval and press on to the board so it is about 8mm ($^{5}/_{16}$in) thick. Shape as shown, with the bottom of the body forming a point, using the template as a guide. Press the baked upper arms and thighs in position and shape the clay to fit.

5 **Boots** These are suitable for Victorian and Edwardian styles. Form each foot into the shape of an ankle boot with rounded toes and mark the boot upper just below the calf. You can vary the upper by marking on laces, adding buttons down the side, or marking small triangles to suggest elastic-sided boots.

6 **Finishing the feet** Measure the leg against the template and trim to length. Make a hole about 6mm ($^{1}/_{4}$in) deep in the top. The angle behind the knee is cut after baking to avoid distorting the foot.

7 **Baking** Bake all the limb pieces for 25 minutes.

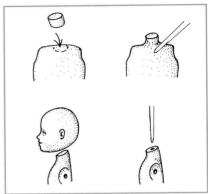

2 **Arm and leg holes** Pierce right through the upper body with the wool needle for arm holes, using the impression from the upper arms as a guide to the position of the hole. Make two leg holes, piercing upwards 6mm ($^{1}/_{4}$in) deep into the body and using the impressions as a guide.

3 **Neck** Cut a 5mm ($^{3}/_{16}$in) slice from a 5mm ($^{3}/_{16}$in) thick log for the neck and press on to the top of the body. Smooth the join into the shoulders with the side of the wool needle. Press the baked head on to the neck, trimming the neck to the correct angle Make a hole in the neck where the hole in the head has left an impression, taking care that the body arm hole remains open.

4 **Baking** Bake the body for 20 minutes.

Assembly Instructions for assembly are on page 46.

Sculpting Baby Dolls

These are made in a different way to the other dolls because pipe cleaners are too large for jointing such tiny dolls. The arms and legs are jointed at the shoulder and hip only using jewellery head pins or wire. These instructions are for a baby of about one year old but you can easily make smaller babies by adjusting the size.

THE HEAD

1 Form a 13mm (½in) ball of clay. Shape it a little so that the side view is like the drawing at the top right. Gently press the side of a pencil into the clay about half way up the front (not too deeply). Form a 1.5mm (¹⁄₁₆in) ball and shape it into a teardrop. Press this into the indentation as shown, point upwards, and smooth in the edges with the side of the needle until the nose is a button with only a slight rise for the bridge.

BABY DOLL TEMPLATE
Actual size template and assembly diagram of the baby doll.

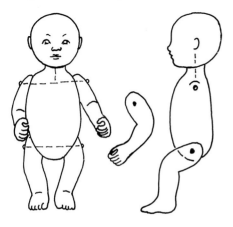

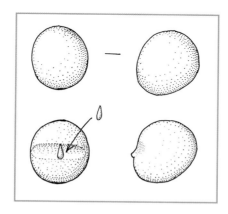

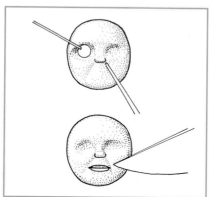

2 Make shallow impressions for the eye sockets with the ball-headed pin tool. Make two shallow indentations on either side of the mouth area as shown, running down from the nose. Make a cut for the mouth about 2mm (³⁄₃₂in) below the bottom of the nose and open it with your knife.

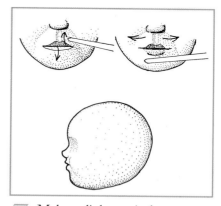

3 Make a slight vertical groove on the top lip and stroke upwards with the side of the wool needle to shape the upper lip. Smooth the cut edge of the bottom lip downwards. Make a horizontal indentation below the mouth to emphasize the bottom lip and smooth away any hard edges. Baby chins are usually very rounded – check the profile but only add more clay for the chin if absolutely necessary.

Use a darning needle to make all the baby limb and body holes (apart from the neck holes) which need to be wide enough to take 0.6mm jewellery head pins or wire. Use the 2mm (³⁄₃₂in) wool needle for the neck holes.

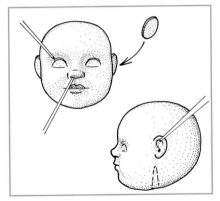

4 Draw in the upper eyelid curve and make another line just above it. The eyes should be small and one eye width apart. Very lightly suggest the bottom eye line. Cut two thin slices from a 3mm (⅛in) log for the ears and apply centrally to the sides of the head. Smooth in the sides towards the face and indent the centres with the ball tool. Draw an 'S'-shaped curve on each ear and make an ear hole at the base of the 'S'. Make a hole with the 2mm (³⁄₃₂in) wool needle centrally underneath the head where the neck will go. Bake the head for 20 minutes.

SCALE

The babies in the photographs on these pages are shown larger than actual size so that you can see the detail. To keep your dolls to scale, be sure to use the template on page 41.

THE ARMS

1 Each arm is made in one piece. Form a 4mm (⁵⁄₃₂in) log of clay and cut two pieces 20mm (¾in) long. Pinch all the cut ends into a rounded shape. Thin the wrists about 5mm (³⁄₁₆in) from the end by rolling the log between your forefingers. Flatten the resulting ball on to the board until it is about 1.5mm (¹⁄₁₆in) thick, flatter towards the end. Flatten the other hand next to the first so you can work on both together to keep them symmetrical, reversing the shaping for the second arm and hand.

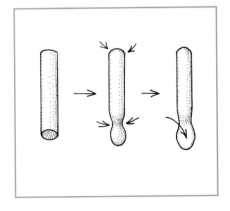

2 Cut away a V section with your knife to make a mitten shape. Cut a line in the centre of the finger area, then make a cut on either side of this to make evenly spaced fingers. Trim the fingers as shown. Use the blade of your knife and your tiny tools to round each fingertip, then mark nails using the eye of a needle. Smooth away any cut edges. Slice off the board and push the thumb downwards. Curve the fingers round into a little fist and accentuate the wrist. Hold the side of a fine needle against the inside of each elbow and bend the arm round this, curving it into a natural shape.

THE BODY

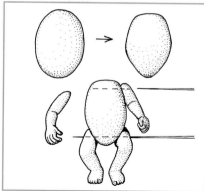

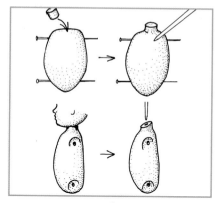

1 Form a 15mm ($^5/_8$in) ball of clay. Shape into an oval and flatten it slightly to make it 13mm ($^1/_2$in) thick. Shape as shown, using the template as a guide and keeping the shape simple and rounded. Lay it on the board and lightly press on the unbaked arms and legs, adjusting them to look realistic. Now pierce right through the arms and body and then the legs and body with a darning needle. Carefully remove the limbs and insert a pin in each body hole to keep it open.

2 Cut a 4mm ($^5/_{32}$in) slice from a 4mm ($^5/_{32}$in) log for the neck and press on to the top of the body. Smooth the join into the shoulders with the side of the wool needle. Press the baked head on to the neck, trimming the neck so that it is very short. Make a 5mm ($^3/_{16}$in) deep hole in the neck with the 2mm ($^3/_{32}$in) needle where the hole in the head has left an impression. Bake the body and limb pieces for 20 minutes. Remove the pins.

Assembly Instructions for assembly are on page 47.

THE LEGS

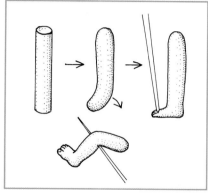

Each leg is also made in one piece. Form a 4mm ($^5/_{32}$in) log of clay and cut two lengths of 25mm (1in). Round the ends as for the arms. Pull down a heel 5mm ($^3/_{16}$in) from one end of each and flatten the little foot on the board. Mark toes with the point of your knife and toenails with the eye of a needle. Slice off the board and make an indentation for the instep. Bend the leg into the shape shown in the template by pressing a fine needle behind the knee and then bending. Repeat for the second leg, reversing the shaping.

CHAPTER 4

ASSEMBLING THE DOLLS

Once all the doll parts have been sculpted and baked, it is time to assemble the doll into a little person. I always find this part of making the dolls enormous fun as it is when they begin to become 'alive'. This chapter lists all the materials you will need to assemble your dolls, then shows you how to put them together into posable little people.

The dolls in this book have a method of jointing that I have developed from techniques used for simple marionettes. It means that the dolls can be posed very naturally. Ordinary pipe cleaners are threaded through the holes in the limbs and body and glued into place in the tops of the forearms and lower legs. The baby dolls are jointed with jewellery wire as they are too small for pipe cleaners.

TOOLS AND MATERIALS FOR ASSEMBLING THE DOLLS

Pipe Cleaners

These are used for assembling the dolls so that they are posable. Flesh-coloured pipe cleaners are available from hobby and doll-making suppliers but the ordinary white or cream ones will serve just as well as they are rarely visible when the doll is finished.

Jewellery Head Pins or Jewellery Wire

These are used for the baby dolls which are too tiny to joint using pipe cleaners. They are available from bead or craft shops. Head pins are lengths of wire with a small head attached and 35mm ($1\frac{3}{8}$in) is the best length to use. These are ideal as the head end will not pull through the holes in the clay and you only need to glue the other end to fix the limbs in place. Alternatively, you can use 0.6mm jewellery wire. You will need two head pins or about 75mm (3in) of wire for a baby doll.

Knife

Use a sharp craft (X-Acto) knife or scalpel to trim away extra clay from around joints so that they will bend more easily.

Sandpaper and Quilt Wadding (Batting)

I use sandpaper for smoothing out surface irregularities after baking and rounding any cut edges. Grades 400 and 600 grit are the best for polymer clay. Rub sanded surfaces with a piece of quilt wadding (batting) or stiff fabric after sanding to restore the surface patina.

Drill Bits

You can use a small drill bit of the right diameter to make holes in the clay after baking although this is really only possible for 6mm ($\frac{1}{4}$in) deep holes and not for holes right through a limb. First make a small pilot hole with the point of your knife and twist the drill bit in the hole by hand or use a small hobby drill. You can enlarge holes that are too small in the same way.

Wire Cutters

These are used to trim the pipe cleaners to the correct length. You can use an old pair of scissors instead but they need to be fairly sturdy.

Glue

The best glue to use for doll assembly is Superglue. This is the rapid-setting cyanoacrylate glue and is used to glue the pipe cleaner or wire ends into the limbs, to glue two pieces of clay together, or to glue clay to hard materials like metal. It gives a very strong bond almost instantly but as it also does the same to human flesh, you need to approach it with some respect.

To glue the pipe cleaners into the holes in the doll's limbs or body, apply a drop of glue to the end of the pipe cleaner and push this firmly into the hole. Excess glue will stiffen the pipe cleaner so be very sparing.

PREPARING THE DOLL PARTS FOR ASSEMBLY

Refer to the complete doll template for the type of doll you are assembling.

- Woman doll on page 19.
- Man doll on page 27.
- Child doll on page 36.
- Baby doll on page 41.

Arrange the baked, sculpted parts of the doll on the template and check that all the parts are the right size. Trim away any excess clay from around the joints and sand them smooth. Be sure to support the clay as you cut or it may snap.

You can correct most mistakes in sculpting at this point. Trim legs to the same length, for example, or cut and sand joints so they bend sufficiently.

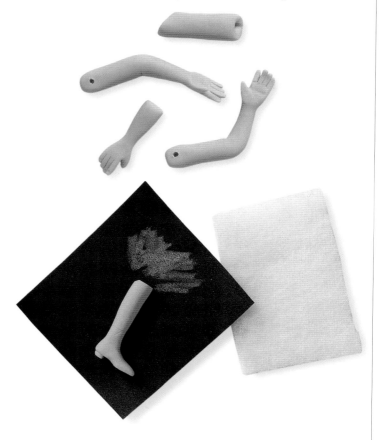

ASSEMBLING AN ADULT OR CHILD DOLL

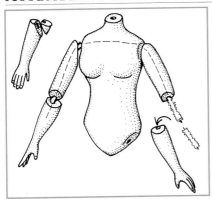

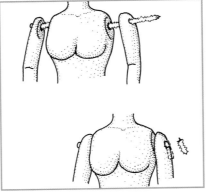

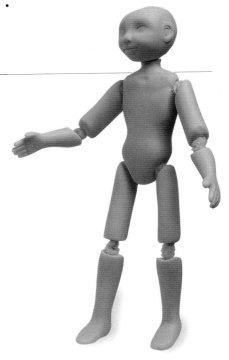

1 **The arms** Cut the inside elbow of each lower arm at a 45° angle and sand smooth. Push a pipe cleaner through the upper body hole and thread on the upper arms. Trim the pipe cleaner to leave 6mm (¼in) at each end for inserting into the forearm holes and allowing a small gap between each body part for movement. Gently push on the forearms, check for free movement and trim away any extra clay if necessary. Finally, glue the two ends of the pipe cleaner into the holes in the forearms.

2 **Woman doll's Regency arms** Glue one end of a pipe cleaner into the hole in the top of the right arm, pass the pipe cleaner through the upper body hole and then through the hole in the left arm. Bend the pipe cleaner down on to the arm, holding everything tight, and apply glue to the pipe cleaner where it emerges from the arm. When it has set, clip off the excess pipe cleaner.

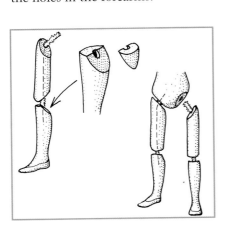

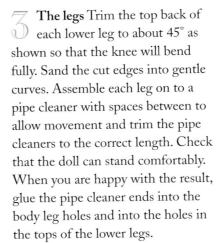

3 **The legs** Trim the top back of each lower leg to about 45° as shown so that the knee will bend fully. Sand the cut edges into gentle curves. Assemble each leg on to a pipe cleaner with spaces between to allow movement and trim the pipe cleaners to the correct length. Check that the doll can stand comfortably. When you are happy with the result, glue the pipe cleaner ends into the body leg holes and into the holes in the tops of the lower legs.

4 **The head** Insert a short length of pipe cleaner into the head hole and trim it so that the head rests on the neck when the other end is inserted into the neck hole. Glue the ends of the pipe cleaner into the holes sparingly so that glue does not get on to the neck surfaces and the head remains free to turn and bend slightly.

ASSEMBLING A BABY DOLL

The baby doll is too tiny to use pipe cleaners for the limbs so is assembled using head pins or jewellery wire.

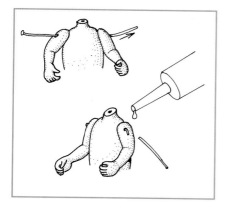

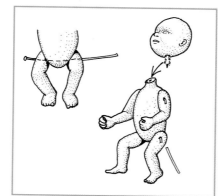

1 Thread a head pin through one arm, through the armhole in the body and then the other arm. Pull the pin taught, fold the end down against the outside of the second arm and apply a drop of glue. Allow to dry, ensuring the glue does not seep into the hole and stick the joint. Clip off the excess. If you are using wire, you will need to glue the first end into the first armhole, then proceed as for the head pins.

2 Repeat for the legs. The head pins or wire should be loose enough to allow movement but not too loose. The head is attached with a short piece of pipe cleaner as for the other dolls (see page 46).

see page 46

POSING THE DOLLS

The adult and child dolls are designed so that they can bend at all the main limb joints and can be posed. To sit the doll, bend the legs up at the hip and down at the knees. You will be able to bend the arms into many different poses so that the dolls look as though they are carrying things, reaching out or gesturing. Try curving the sculpted hand around an object before baking; you can then glue the object into the doll's hand after baking.

The dolls can be made to stand firmly. For this, it is best to put a small piece of Blu-Tak or doll's house wax (available from doll's house shops) on to the bottom of the doll's feet. The feet can now be pressed on to the floor of the doll's house or room box and the rest of the doll posed into a natural position. For the general-purpose display of miniature dolls, you can buy doll stands from doll materials suppliers.

The baby dolls will sit well. Simply push their legs upwards until they sit upright.

CHAPTER 5

PAINTING THE DOLLS

Once the doll has been sculpted, baked and assembled, you will need to paint the face and footwear. Baked flesh-coloured polymer clay has a matt surface that resembles human skin so it is only the facial details and coloured footwear that need painting.

Painting the face is a particularly important part of doll-making and one that is well worth practising to get the best results. A well-painted face can transform a doll and often correct an imperfectly sculpted face. The following instructions will guide you through the painting techniques for different types of face and you will find that you can make any number of variations to add character.

MATERIALS

Paints

Use good-quality artists' acrylic paints such as Winsor and Newton. Oil-based paints should not be used on polymer clay as they may not dry properly, while water colours are not permanent enough. Some cheap hobby paints may bleed into the surrounding clay and are best avoided.

Acrylic paints are versatile and can be used with great delicacy for painting tiny faces. They can be applied as a thin wash to alter flesh tones or suggest tanning, for blushing cheeks and reddening noses. Used thickly they can simulate leather footwear. If you make a mistake, the paint can be wiped or scraped off the clay so you can try again.

Brushes

Use good quality artists' brushes in tiny sizes for applying the paint. Synthetic fibre, round brushes, size 00 to 0000 are best for tiny faces; use larger brushes (size 3 or 4) for painting shoes. Wash brushes thoroughly after use as acrylic paint left in the bristles will soon ruin them. Use larger-size brushes for varnish, and again clean them well after use.

Mixing Palette

The quantities of mixed paint required for tiny faces are so small that a piece of card or a small saucer is all you will need as a mixing surface.

Powder Colours

These can be brushed on to either unbaked or baked clay to colour cheeks and give other subtle colour effects. They are hard to remove from unbaked clay if you make a mistake so it is easier to apply them to baked clay. The best to use are soft artists' pastels from art shops. Rub them on to paper to release the powder which is then brushed on to the clay with a paintbrush. Varnish with matt varnish to stop the colour rubbing off. Avoid using eye make-up colours as these may discolour in time.

Metallic powders, often sold with the clays or in art shops, are excellent for simulating brass, gold or silver buttons and accessories. Brush on to soft clay and after baking, then varnish with a gloss varnish.

Varnishes

Matt varnish is used as a protection and/or barrier for paint. Gloss varnish can be used to give painted footwear a shine if required. It can also be used on the doll's eyes to make them shine but I prefer to use a dot of white for this effect as it is more controllable at this scale.

The best varnishes are spirit-based and water-based varnishes sold by the clay manufacturers in both matt and gloss. The spirit-based varnish is the most resilient and brushes should be cleaned with methylated spirit (denatured alcohol). Acrylic varnishes can also be used, but do not use oil-based varnishes which will not dry on baked polymer clay. Transparent nail varnish can also be unstable on polymer clay.

Methylated Spirits (Denatured Alcohol)

This is used for de-greasing the surface before applying acrylic paint and for washing brushes after using spirit-based varnish. Nail varnish remover is an alternative.

PAINTING THE FACES

For all faces, it is advisable to apply a thin coat of matt varnish to create a barrier between the baked polymer clay and the paint. This will prevent any bleeding of colours into the clay, which can happen some time after painting. Be sure to use matt varnish and stir or shake the pot thoroughly before use, otherwise the varnish will have a slight gloss. When the varnish is dry, brush the surface lightly with methylated spirits to de-grease it so that the paint will adhere firmly.

You can now begin to paint the face. If you make a mistake, wipe the paint off before it dries and try again. To remove dried paint, scrape gently with a blunt knife blade, then rub the surface with methylated spirits to remove any residue.

Colours

The following colours are used for painting faces:

- **White** For mixing with any colour for lightening and also for the whites of eyes.
- **Crimson** Used in mixtures for cheeks and lips.
- **Dark brown** For outlining eyes and painting brows.
- **Black** For pupils and to darken blues and greens.
- **Blue, green and brown** For the irises of eyes.
- **Yellow** Used for mixing into lip colour for a more peachy result and for adding to eye colour for variation.

Eye Colours

- **Blue eyes** Blue, a touch of black and lightened with a little white
- **Green eyes** Green, a touch of brown and lightened with a little white.
- **Brown eyes** Any warm brown paint such as Burnt Umber with a little white or yellow.
- **Grey eyes** White, black and a touch of blue or green.
- **Hazel eyes** Brown, yellow and a touch of green.

Lip Colours

- **Women and children** Crimson with touch of yellow. Use the paint diluted into a thin wash.
- **Men** As above but with a little brown added.
- **Women with lipstick** Crimson with a touch of white for cool reds. Add yellow for more scarlet-coloured lips.

Cheek Colours

Use a watery version of the natural lip colour and rub in with your finger to avoid hard edges. Alternatively brush on red powder colour.

PAINTING A YOUNG WOMAN'S FACE

 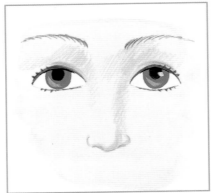 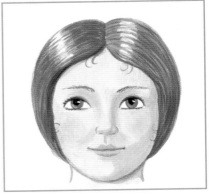

1 Eyes Using dark brown paint, draw a fine line along the top of each eyelid. Mix an eye colour (see page 49) and paint two circles in the centre of each eye, letting the upper eyelid cut off the top of the circles as shown. Paint a black dot for the pupil in the centre of the eye, just touching the upper lid line, and make a tiny line of black above the coloured iris, just under the eye line, to suggest shadow. Paint a streak of a lighter version of the eye colour round one side of each eye.

2 Eyebrows and eyelashes Paint tiny triangles of white in the corners of the eyes. Thin some dark brown paint and paint in the eyebrows as a series of tiny strokes, feathering along the brow. If you are right handed, the doll's right eyebrow will be hardest to do so paint this first, then paint the left one to match. Paint a few tiny, dark brown dots along the upper eyelid as shown to suggest long lashes. A few tiny strokes along the bottom of the eye will suggest lower lashes but use this with discretion. Finally paint a tiny dot of white as shown to give a shine.

3 Lips and cheeks Mix a lip colour (see page 49) and paint the sculpted lips with a thin wash, allowing the paint to seep into the central crack to darken it. Allow to dry, then repeat until the colour is deep enough. Finally paint the cheeks by wetting a finger and dipping it into diluted lip colour. Apply the paint sparingly, rubbing it into the cheekbone area with your fingertip and wiping off if it is too strong. An alternative for cheeks is to brush on a rosy powder colour after baking.

4 Varnish The paint is unlikely to rub off unless the doll is to be handled a lot, in which case you can apply matt varnish again to protect it when the paint is dry.

VARIATIONS FOR DIFFERENT DOLLS' FACES

The instructions opposite are for a basic woman's face and you will find you can vary expression and colouring considerably with your painting. Eye colour is the most obvious variable but you can use darker paint for the eye lines of a darker doll, lighter for a fair doll and so on. Eyebrows can be arched or straight, fine or heavy, high or low and can vary the look considerably.

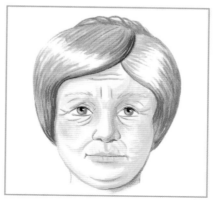

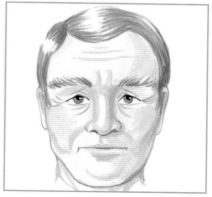

Old Woman A slightly faded look works well, so keep the colours muted. Eyebrows can be slightly rougher than for the young woman and with grey streaks. Bright lipstick and rouged cheeks can suggest an older lady of spirit! Blue veins will age the backs of hands; paint on thin lines of dilute colour.

Old Man Paint this as for the young man but with grey, bristling brows. A nose and cheeks reddened with washes suggest a man of indulgent tastes. Use a brown wash on the face, neck and hands for a weather-beaten look.

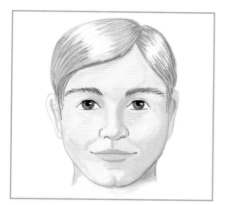

Young Man Paint the top eye line more angular and the brows heavier. The lips should be very subtle in colour and look best with a little brown mixed into the wash. Do not suggest lashes, although darker men can have a light line along the bottom of the eye. Blue-black powder colour can be brushed on to suggest stubble.

Child This is similar to the young woman doll. Keep brow lines fine, cheeks rosy and lips natural. A sprinkle of freckles across the nose adds character.

Baby Keep the eyes and mouth fairly small. Use light brown for the eye lines and a tiny suggestion only of eyebrows. The coloured iris should be quite large in the eye. Lips should be natural and cheeks rosy.

PAINTING FOOTWEAR

The following acrylic paint colours are used for painting the footwear: white, dark brown, black, gold and various colours for coloured stockings and shoes.

The following are useful colours mixtures. When mixing, always start with the lighter colour and gradually add the darker one until you have the shade you want.

- **Light brown** Made with a mixture of dark brown and white.
- **Grey** Made with a mixture of white with a small amount of black.

After baking, brush the shoe area with methylated spirits to degrease the surface. If the doll has socks or stockings, paint these first, applying two coats of thick acrylic paint. Allow the dry, then paint the shoe, again with two coats, covering the soles and the shoe uppers and keeping the top line as neat as you can. You can pick out laces and buttons as necessary when the basic colour is dry. A coat of matt varnish will protect the paint and a light polish with a little furniture polish will give the effect of shiny leather.

Tudor Shoes

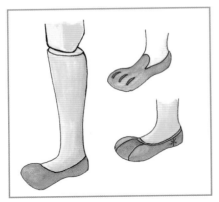

Men's legs should be left flesh-coloured as they will wear fabric hose. Paint the legs of women and girl dolls white or in a bright colour for stockings. For all dolls, paint the shoes light brown. You can add slashes or lacing details if you wish.

Regency Shoes

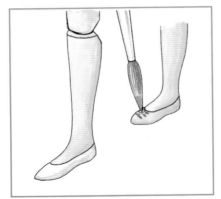

For women and girls Paint the simple slippers white or in a colour to match the clothes, as shoes were sometimes made of matching silk. You can paint in some tiny coloured details to suggest embroidery. The legs should be left unpainted.

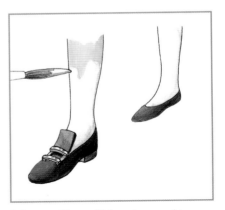

Men and boys Paint the stockings white and the shoes black. Pick out the men's buckles in gold paint. This is easier to do if you hold the edge of a piece of paper against the buckle to mask the black paint.

Victorian Boots

Boots for all were black or brown. Men's and boys' stockings were mostly black or grey. Women and girls wore white or coloured stockings to match their outfit.

Edwardian Boots and Shoes

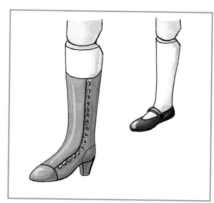

Women Paint stockings white and the high-buttoned boots in black, light brown or grey. Pick out the buttons in a darker tone.

Girls Black ankle-strap shoes and white socks or stockings. Gloss varnish on the shoes gives the effect of patent leather.

Men Shoes brown or black and sometimes two-tone brown and white; socks or stockings in sober matching colours.

Boys Black boots and black or grey stockings or socks.

CHAPTER 6

SEWING MATERIALS AND TECHNIQUES

Sewing clothes for miniature dolls is a delightful occupation and it is extremely satisfying to make clothes for dolls that you have made yourself. Provided that you have kept to the template sizes when making your dolls, all the patterns in this book should fit your tiny people with little adjustment. You will need only basic sewing skills and all the clothes can be hand sewn if you do not have a sewing machine.

If you want to use the patterns to make clothes for purchased dolls, they should fit well provided that the dolls are a standard 1:12 scale.

THE CLOTHES

The miniature clothes in this book have all been carefully designed to be historically accurate for their periods, allowing for limitations of scale. All have been adapted from contemporary paintings and photographs or period clothes in museums. My prime concern has been that the clothes should look as realistic as possible but still be simple to make. Some parts of garments are omitted to avoid bulk – the backs of waistcoats and shirt sleeves, for example – while women's and girl's underclothes are kept to a minimum.

The clothes are not intended to be removable as this tends to sacrifice appearance and fit. If you wish to make removable clothes, you can adapt the patterns but you will need to make the clothes looser.

SOURCES OF MATERIALS

Choosing materials for the costumes is part of the delight! As you need such small quantities you can acquire a wonderful collection of fabrics and trims at very little cost. A good source of fabrics and trimmings specifically chosen for miniature dolls is the various specialist mail order firms that sell doll's house haberdashery and fabric and these advertise in doll's house magazines. Charity shops are excellent sources for old, well-washed fabric, which has a soft texture ideal for working on a small scale.

FABRICS

Scale is an important consideration when choosing fabric for miniature dolls. At the scale of 1:12, a fine lawn is actually about as thick as a piece of sacking! This means that all fabrics are going to be a compromise as it is impossible to obtain fabrics that are truly to scale. If you wish to achieve some semblance of realism, you will need to choose the finest possible fabrics for miniature dolls' clothes. Avoid stiff and bulky fabrics and those which have thick fibres and an open weave.

The following list gives the types of fabric that I have found most successful when making miniature dolls' clothes.

Plain Cotton

Use lightweight fabrics in a fine weave. This is the easiest type of fabric to use for miniature clothes and one to be recommended for beginners. It does not fray badly, it comes in a wonderful range of colours and prints, and if it is washed first to remove any dressing, it also drapes well. Patchwork fabrics are a useful source of tiny florals, checks and tartans.

Polycotton

This is available in very fine weaves and plain or printed. It does not drape as well as pure cotton.

Cotton Lawn

This is a very fine fabric and usually plain white or pastel coloured. It is ideal for underclothes and men's shirts. A good source of white lawn is lace-trimmed lawn handkerchiefs, especially well-washed ones – and you can use the lace as well!

Cotton Voile

A fine, soft and sheer fabric that drapes well, it is usually available in white only. It is good for under-clothes, babies' bonnets and nappies (diapers), blouses and any use requiring a delicate, sheer fabric. Thin white lawn is an alternative.

Cotton Corduroy

Only use the very fine cords. These are available from doll's house fabric suppliers. They are used for men's and boys' trousers and jackets.

Cotton Jersey

This is used for hose (stockings) in the Tudor costumes. My favourite source is old T-shirts or women's briefs and you will need the thinnest jersey you can find.

Pure Silk

Available in various weights, silk comes in a wonderful array of colours. It gives a lovely sheen to miniature costumes and once it has been fray-stopped (see page 57) to prevent fraying, is delightful to work with and irons beautifully. Dupion is a heavier silk that makes good jackets, while silk taffeta can sometimes be found in checks and stripes. Jacquard has a patterned weave. Look out for silk scarves and ties in charity shops which often have tiny designs that are perfect for miniature dresses and waistcoats.

Brocade

This luxury fabric often has metallic threads in the weave and is used for Tudor clothes where a touch of 'cloth of gold' is required! It tends to be too stiff to drape so use it for trimmings and cuffs. Choose tiny patterns.

Synthetic Fabrics

These usually do not drape well at such a small scale, although they often have the advantage of not fraying. Do not discount them completely as occasionally you may find a fabric perfect for a particular costume.

TRIMMINGS

The right trimmings will make a costume; the wrong ones will ruin it. This is particularly true when working in miniature, as scale is so crucial. As with the fabrics, we can only ever compromise on the scale

of trimmings as a 13mm ($\frac{1}{2}$in) wide piece of lace would need an equivalent of about 1mm ($\frac{1}{32}$in) wide on your doll. The following list includes trimmings that are available from doll's house haberdashery suppliers but you will be able to find many suitable trimmings in most haberdashery shops.

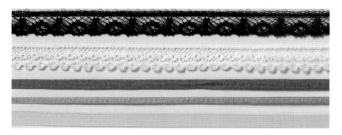

Lace

Choose the narrowest widths you can find, although any fine lace of a suitable design can be cut down. You can also cut out lace motifs to use as collars and spot trims.

Ribbon

This is extremely useful for trimming, edging, bows, sashes and ties. Pure silk ribbon is not expensive and it is the best to use as it will curl and drape beautifully. It is available in a wonderful variety of colours and comes in several narrow widths: 2mm ($\frac{3}{32}$in) and 3mm ($\frac{1}{8}$in) widths are the most useful, although wider ribbon is good for sashes and cravats. Organdie ribbon is lovely for trimming hats and making 'big' bows, while velvet ribbon makes a rich trim for dresses and Tudor clothes.

Braids

There are many narrow braids available from doll's house haberdashers and it is fun to keep a selection. Braid will curve into loops and go round corners so it is good for trimming round necklines and corners. Soutache braid comes in 1mm ($\frac{1}{32}$in) and 2mm ($\frac{3}{32}$in) widths and a good range of colours. If you pull up one of the side threads, it will gather into a wavy trimming.

Picot Braid

This comes as single (one edge with picot loops) or double (both edges with picots) and is 3mm ($\frac{1}{8}$in) wide. It is an attractive trim, available in lots of colours that often match the soutache.

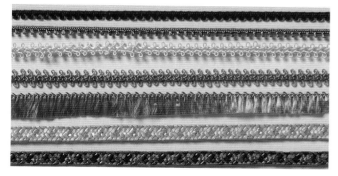

Fringe

This is difficult to find in very narrow widths but you can make your own by cutting off one long edge of a length of silk ribbon and fraying it.

Hat Straw

This comes in a variety of colours but the natural and straw colours usually look best. The 5mm ($\frac{3}{16}$in) width is used in the projects.

OTHER MATERIALS

You will need tracing paper, pencil and double-sided sticky tape for making your patterns (see page 60).

Marking Pencil

You can use a proprietary marking pen with disappearing ink for transferring pattern markings to the fabric. An alternative is a well-sharpened artists' pastel pencil, available in many colours from art shops, that will mark even the dark fabrics successfully but brushes off when you have finished.

Sewing Thread

Polyester thread is finer than cotton so it shows less. Try to match the thread to the fabric as closely as possible. If you are using a machine, be sure to use the same colour thread in the bobbin.

Tissue Paper

Use this for machine-sewing tiny garments (see page 60).

Bonded Interlining

The lightweight iron-on kind can be used for stiffening as required.

Bonding Web

An iron-on webbing in a strip, this is invaluable for bonding two pieces of fabric and turning up hems.

Fray-stop

You can buy little bottles of this under various brand names. To use, squeeze a little on to a saucer and use a fine paintbrush to paint a thin line along all the cut edges of fabric before you sew. Set the pieces aside to dry. This will prevent any fraying and is particularly useful for silk. The painted edges will be hidden inside the garment or covered with trim. Wash your brush in methylated spirit (denatured alcohol) after use.

Glue

Use a PVA fabric glue for gluing fabric – my favourite is Aleene's Tacky Glue which dries clear and flexible. Non-PVA glues may stain badly in time. You can buy a glue syringe from doll's house suppliers for applying tiny quantities of glue in the right place. Use a fast-setting glue such as UHU for making roses and hats.

TRIMMINGS TO MAKE

Buttons

These are easy to make with polymer clay. You will need coloured polymer clay, a ceramic tile and a darning needle.

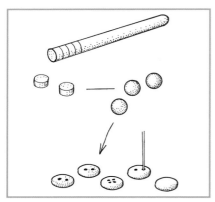

1 Form a 1.5mm ($\frac{1}{16}$in) thick log of clay and cut plenty of 1.5mm ($\frac{1}{16}$in) lengths. Form each length into a ball and press down on to the tile so that it sticks and forms a little button. Try to keep all the buttons the same size. Now pierce each one with the darning needle either with two holes or four. If you want shank-effect buttons, do not pierce. Bake on the tile and remove when cool.

2 For brass or silver buttons, brush with metallic powder before baking, bake and then varnish. You can make buttons in any colour to match the clothes by mixing the clay. Buttons are glued on with a dab of PVA glue, but if you are very dedicated, they can be sewn on!

Bows

These are always useful for hair, hats and clothes. You can buy bow-makers from specialist shops but it is just as simple to use polymer clay and two needles.

To make a perfect 6mm ($\frac{1}{4}$in) bow, push two needles into a lump of clay about 6mm ($\frac{1}{4}$in) apart. Wrap a length of ribbon round as shown, tie a knot in the centre and slip off the needles. Turn the bow round for the neatest side, trim the ends to length and stop them fraying with a dab of glue.

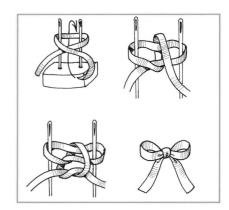

Gathered Rosettes

Use these for hats and shoes.

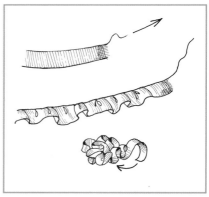

Take a length of 2mm ($\frac{3}{32}$in) wide ribbon. Find the end of a longitudinal thread and pull up to gather into a pretty frill. Use this as a trim or gather further and curl it into a rosette. Tuck under the ends and stitch or glue in place.

Ribbon Roses

These are perfect for trimming bonnets and hats but they can be used for spot trims on bodices and skirts as well. You can buy a rose-maker from doll's house haberdashers but it is easy to make one.

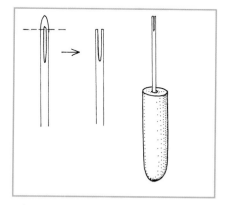

1 You will need a needle with a large eye such as a darning needle, a file and some polymer clay. File off the top of the eye as shown. Form a log of clay and insert the point of the needle well into it. Bake for 30 minutes.

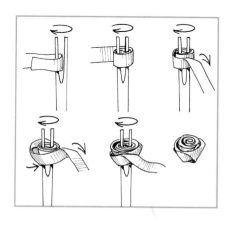

2 To make the roses, use pure silk or organdie ribbon 3–5mm ($\frac{1}{8}$–$\frac{3}{16}$in) wide and quick-setting glue such as UHU. Fold a loop in the end of a length of ribbon and slip it over the needle between the prongs. Rotate the tool a few times to wind in the end of the ribbon and secure with a dab of glue. Apply more glue to the bottom edge of the ribbon, fold the ribbon outwards and down and press on to the glue, pulling it tight at the base and leaving it more open at the top.

Repeat, working round the rose, applying glue and folding the ribbon over until the rose is large enough. Cut the end and glue under the rose. Allow to dry and slip off the needle. You can glue on a snippet of green ribbon as a leaf.

SEWING THE CLOTHES

These techniques for making miniature clothes involve a mixture of sewing, bonding and gluing. I have kept them as simple as possible so that even a beginner can attempt them with confidence. The following tips should help you to achieve the best possible results and make clothes that look wonderful!

- Always iron your fabric and trimmings before you start if they show any creases. Iron the little garments after each step; the instructions will tell you when to do this. I find that for such small clothes, a towel folded on a table top near to where I am sewing is a perfect mini ironing board.
- Keep a pair of dressmaking scissors purely for making your dolls' clothes and always keep them as sharp as possible.
- All the patterns have a 3mm (⅛in) seam allowance.
- If you have made your doll fatter or taller than the template in the sculpting instructions, you will need to adjust your pattern accordingly.
- After cutting out, transfer all the pattern markings to the fabric with a marker pen or pencil and paint the cut edges with fray-stop.
- You can use a sewing machine for sewing seams and gathering, but as tiny pieces of fabric can be dragged into the machine's footplate while sewing, you will need to use a paper shield. Place a piece of tissue paper over the footplate and sew the fabric on this. After sewing, carefully tear away the paper. Use fine machine needles.
- If you sew by hand, use a backstitch and tiny stitches for seams, keeping your line of stitching as straight as possible.

You will need to know the following basic techniques before you attempt any of the sewing projects. They will be used constantly in the projects and are covered here to avoid repetition.

CUTTING TECHNIQUES

Cutting Out

It is difficult to keep tiny patterns in place on the fabric while you cut out, but pins buckle the paper and fabric. An easy solution is to back the patterns with double-sided sticky tape.

Trace the pattern parts that you need, including all the markings, on to tracing paper. Stick double-sided tape over the back of the traced patterns and, leaving the backing strip in place, cut them out. Remove the backing strip on the tape and press the sticky side down on to some fabric a few times so that it becomes a little less tacky. Now you can position your pattern pieces on the fabric and they will stay in place while you cut round them. Store the pattern pieces on a piece of polythene to prevent them sticking to each other.

Cutting on the Fold

This instruction on the patterns means that you should fold the fabric in half, either along the grain or on the cross (see page 61). Lay the side of the pattern marked 'fold' along the exact edge of the fold and cut out through the two thicknesses.

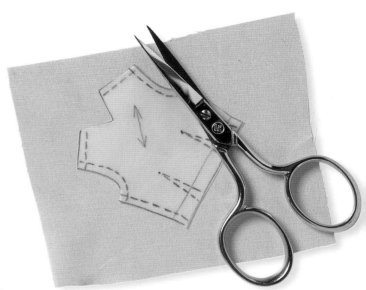

Cutting on the Cross

This is an invaluable technique for making miniature clothes as it results in the fabric having a slight horizontal and vertical stretch which makes fitting far easier. The symbol of a diagonal arrow on a pattern piece indicates it should be cut on the cross. To do this, find the grain of the fabric by examining it closely – you will see that one lot of threads run in one direction while the others are woven at right angles to them. Align the arrow on the pattern parallel to either of these directions and cut out.

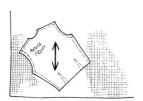 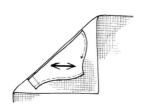

If you are cutting a pattern piece on a fold and on the cross, first fold the fabric along a diagonal of 45° to the weave, then lay the pattern piece on the fold and cut out.

Where there is no arrow on a pattern piece, this means you should align the sides of the pattern along the straight grain.

Cutting Four Pieces

The patterns will sometimes tell you to 'Cut 4'. This is used for waistcoats, coats and jackets when the front of the coat will be made double to provide a facing. To cut four, fold the fabric to double it, allowing for cutting on the cross if required, and cut out two pairs of fronts. Each pair will then be stitched together and turned to give a neat front edge for the garment.

STITCHES

The following hand stitches are used in the projects.

Backstitch

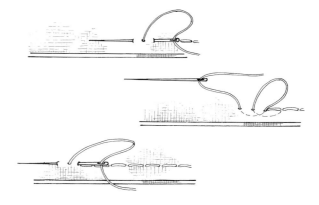

A strong stitch used for seams if you do not have a sewing machine. Knot the end of the thread and bring the needle up from the wrong side of the fabric. Insert the needle 1.5mm ($\frac{1}{16}$in) behind the point where the thread emerges and bring it up the same distance beyond. Repeat, always inserting the needle into the front hole of the previous stitch. Use very tiny stitches and sew in as straight a line as you can.

Slip Stitch

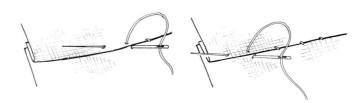

Slipstitch is used for closing the back seam, stitching a bodice to a skirt or for attaching trimmings. The longer stitch passes under the fabric with only a tiny stitch on the surface to catch the fabric down.

Ladder Stitch

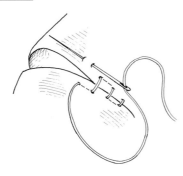

This is used for attaching sleeves. Make several stitches as shown, spacing them evenly like the rungs of a ladder. Pull up to close the two sides, pushing the raw edges of the fabric to the back.

Running Stitch

This is a simple in-and-out stitch of equal length above and below the fabric. It is used for gathering.

SEWING TECHNIQUES

Darts

These are used to shape a bodice to the doll's body and their positions are marked on the patterns. After cutting out, transfer the markings to the fabric very accurately. With right sides together, fold the fabric along the centre of the dart, aligning the stitching lines carefully. Stitch from the wide end towards the point and finish by stitching right over the edge of the folded fabric and securing. Press the dart to one side.

Clipping Curves and Corners

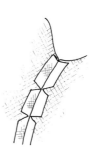

Any seam that is sewn on a curve should have the seam allowance clipped just up to the stitching line as shown. Then, when the seam is pressed open, it will lie flat. You will also need to clip across any corners and when the piece is turned to the right side, use the point of your scissors or a blunt needle to push out the corner carefully from inside to make it pointed.

Turning

After sewing sleeves and trousers legs, they will need turning to the right side. My favourite way of doing this is to attach a safety pin to the narrowest end of the sleeve or leg and poke this through, pulling the rest of the piece through to the right side.

Gathering

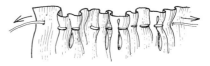

Lines of gathering are indicated on the patterns. For hand sewing, sew a line of running stitch (simple in-and-out stitch) just into the seam allowance, pull up as necessary and stitch to hold. If you are machining, use a large-size stitch and sew two lines of gathers. Pull up the threads as necessary, holding them by knotting them together or winding them round a pin placed across each end of the line of gathering. Tiny sections of gathering around the tops of sleeves or around wrists are best done by hand on the doll.

Inserting Sleeves

Tiny sleeves are best inserted on the doll. This technique is a little tricky the first time you try it but you will soon improve and you will get a far neater result than if you sew the sleeves to the bodice before fitting to the doll.

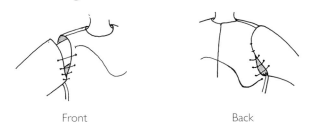

Front   Back

Plain Sleeves Make the sleeves and pull them on to the doll. Align the sleeve underarm seam with the bodice side seam. Starting from the underarm and working first up the front, use ladder stitch to sew the sleeve to the bodice. Use your needle to push the raw edges inwards and try to keep the two sides well aligned. Continue round over the top of the shoulder and down the back, easing the fabric to fit as you go. Finally fasten off at the underarm.

Gathered Sleeves For very full gathered sleeves, such as the Regency woman's dress, gather the sleeve first, then stitch to the bodice using the instructions for a plain sleeve. For other gathered sleeves, it is easiest to gather on the doll.

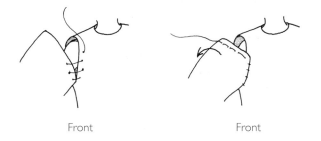

Front   Front

Make the sleeves, omitting any gathering at this point, and pull them on to the doll. Align the underarm seams. Starting at the underarm seam,

ladder stitch as for the plain sleeve until you get to the start of the gathering line. Anchor the thread with a tiny stitch, then run a line of gathering stitches along the gathering line to the end of it.

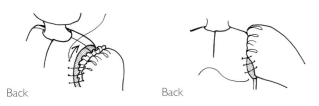

Back   Back

Pull up the gathers until the sleeve fits the armhole perfectly all round. Stitch it to the bodice at this point and now work backwards with ladder stitch to the start of the gathers. Finally ladder stitch the remaining section from the end of the gathers to the underarm. This method ensures that the gathered sleeve fits the armhole accurately.

Hems and Cuffs

There are several ways to finish hems and cuffs in miniature sewing. The prime consideration should be to avoid bulk and hems should always be single (turned up once, not twice). Always finish the hem or cuffs before sewing the garment on to the doll. Check the length by holding the piece against the doll before hemming. With skirts and trousers, you can adjust the height at the waist to a certain extent after the hem has been finished.

Bonded Hem Use this for plain cuffs, trouser legs and straighter skirts. Press up the hem to the height required. Cut a strip of bonding web and lay along the fold. Iron again to hold the hem in place.

Trimmed Hem Use this for cuffs or skirts with an edge of trimming or lace. Cut the hem to the required length and apply a thin line of fabric glue along the bottom edge. Press on the trim, overlapping the ends at the back seam.

Closures

Fold one side over the raw edge of the other and slip stitch the sides together. Alternatively, use a backstitch, placing each visible stitch where a button is to be glued. The slight dent caused by the stitch makes the buttons look very realistic.

Adding Trims

Trims of all kinds can either be sewn in place or glued with fabric glue. Sewing is time-consuming but does avoid the possibility of glue showing or becoming stiff. Gluing is quick and useful around necklines or on tiny bodices where sewing might pucker the material.

Sewing Trims Be sure to keep your stitches as small as possible, use a matching thread and try to keep each stitch invisible from the right side. Use a running or slip stitch and catch the trim to the fabric at approximately 3mm ($^{1}/_{8}$in) intervals.

Gluing Trims To glue a line of trim, squeeze a little PVA glue on to some scrap paper and dip the side of a pin into it. Press the side of the pin on to the fabric to leave a neat line of glue. Repeat as necessary and press on the trim. Wipe away any excess glue immediately and avoid letting glue get on to other areas of fabric. A glue syringe is a useful alternative (see page 57).

THE PATTERNS

All the patterns are drawn actual size. The seam allowance throughout is 3mm ($^{1}/_{8}$in). Hems are usually 5mm ($^{3}/_{16}$in) but may vary. The following symbols are used on the patterns:

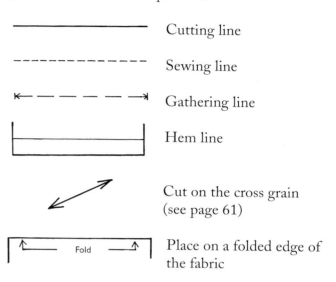

————————	Cutting line
– – – – – – – –	Sewing line
←– – – – – –→	Gathering line
⎴⎽⎽⎽⎽⎽⎴	Hem line
↗ ↙	Cut on the cross grain (see page 61)
⬚ Fold ⬚	Place on a folded edge of the fabric

For each of the projects I have assumed that you have matching thread, needles, scissors, glue, bonding web and fray-stop.

CHAPTER 7

DRESSING THE DOLLS IN TUDOR COSTUME

The Tudor period in the sixteenth century is a popular one with doll's house collectors and the houses are extremely attractive with their half-timbering, heavy wooden furniture, tapestries, tiles and wonderful fireplaces. The costumes are equally sumptuous with rich colours, velvets and brocades. Fashion in clothing varied considerably throughout the Tudor reigns and the costumes given in this section are chosen from the first half of the sixteenth century. In the photograph, a Tudor nobleman and his family gather in their parlour. All the clothes are projects in this chapter.

FABRICS

Reds, golds, yellows and greens were particularly popular as were large all-over patterns of stylized leaf-and-flower motifs. During the reign of Henry VIII, clothes of the nobility became very elaborate and were studded with jewels, while 'cloth of gold' and sumptuous brocades, velvets and silks were worn by all who could afford them.

Tudor Woman's Clothes

The doll wears a typical gown of the period with a square neckline and full sleeves turned back to show a brocade lining. Her headdress is the French hood which was worn by many well-known Tudors including Anne Boleyn and Mary Tudor. It is considered unlikely that women wore anything other than petticoats beneath their gowns at this time but Queen Elizabeth I is known to have worn drawers so I have included some simple drawers as well.

MATERIALS

- Woman doll with Tudor bust and shoes (see pages 19–26)
- Patterns for the Tudor woman's clothes traced and cut out (see page 70)

Drawers
- Cream lawn

Gown
- Red cotton fabric, plain or with a stylized print
- Brocade or patterned silk for the sleeve linings
- 2mm ($^3/_{32}$in) black silk ribbon
- 2mm ($^3/_{32}$in) gold braid
- Gold fringe for tassels
- 6mm ($^1/_4$in) patterned ribbon

Headdress
- Lightweight black cotton fabric
- Interlining
- White single picot braid

Necklace
- Fine beading wire and a tiny bead

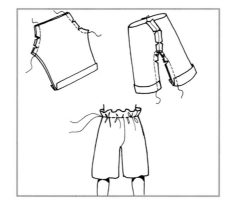

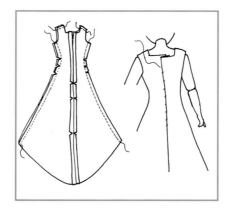

1 **Drawers** Cut out the drawers and fray-stop the edges. Press up a bonded hem on each leg. With right sides together, sew the two body seams. Clip curves, press the seams open, then refold as shown. Sew the leg and crotch seam and clip curves. Turn and pull on to the doll. Run a gathering thread around the waist, pull up to fit and fasten off.

2 **Gown** Cut out the gown in red cotton and the sleeve linings in brocade or silk. Fray-stop all edges. With right sides together, sew the two backs together at the centre back seam as far as the dot. Clip curves and press the seam open. With right sides together, sew the back to the front at the side and shoulder seams. Clip curves and press the seams open. Pull the gown on to the doll and check the bottom hem for length, trimming if necessary – it should trail at the back. Slip stitch the back closure.

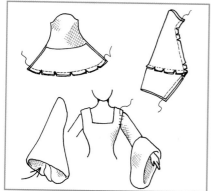

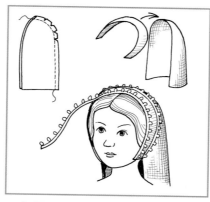

5 **Headdress** Cut out the hood in black fabric and the headdress front in interlined black fabric. Fray-stop the hood edges and sew the centre back seam. Clip curves and press the seam open. Glue the stiffened front to the front of the hood and glue two lengths of picot braid to the front and back of the stiffened front. Glue the headdress to the doll's head, placing it well back on the head and gluing the two fronts round on to the lower cheeks. Arrange the hood to fall behind the shoulders.

3 **Sleeves** With right sides together, sew each sleeve to a sleeve lining along the bottom hem. Clip curves, open out, then fold right sides together as shown. Sew the underarm seams of the sleeves and sleeve linings as one seam. Clip curves, press and turn. Push each sleeve lining into the sleeve. Pull the sleeves on to the doll (the length allows a deep turn back). Ladder stitch each sleeve to the bodice (see page 64). Turn back the cuffs to reveal the lining.

4 **Hair** Wig the doll in the parted upswept style on page 120 without a bun.

DRAWERS
Cut 2 on fold

Fold

GOWN BACK
Cut 2

HOOD
Cut 2

HEADDRESS FRONT
Cut 1

6 **Finishing** Glue a line each of black ribbon and gold braid to the gown neck, covering the raw edges and clipping the neck lower if necessary. Glue a line of patterned ribbon all round the bottom hem. Tie a girdle of braid round the waist to hang loosely and glue a tassel on each made from folded fringe. The necklace is a tiny bead glued into a loop of beading wire which is placed round the neck.

SLEEVE
Cut 2

SLEEVE LINING
Cut 2

GOWN FRONT
Cut 1 on fold

Fold

Tudor Man's Clothes

*The doll wears a doublet which was the standard man's dress,
in various styles, throughout the sixteenth century. Hose, a form of tights,
were always worn with the doublet while a black hat with a white
feather completes the outfit.*

MATERIALS

- Man doll with Tudor shoes
  (see pages 27–33)
- Patterns for the Tudor man's clothes
  traced and cut out
  (see page 72)

Hose
- White cotton jersey
- 2mm (³⁄₃₂in) brown soutache braid

Doublet
- Purple silk
- White lawn for the undershirt
- 2mm (³⁄₃₂in) gold silk ribbon
- Contrasting brocade for the cuffs

Hat
- Black cotton jersey
- Small white feather or
  piece of down

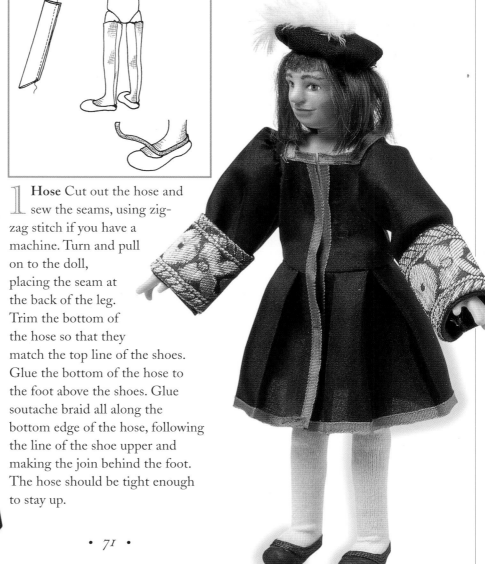

1 Hose Cut out the hose and
sew the seams, using zig-
zag stitch if you have a
machine. Turn and pull
on to the doll,
placing the seam at
the back of the leg.
Trim the bottom of
the hose so that they
match the top line of the shoes.
Glue the bottom of the hose to
the foot above the shoes. Glue
soutache braid all along the
bottom edge of the hose, following
the line of the shoe upper and
making the join behind the foot.
The hose should be tight enough
to stay up.

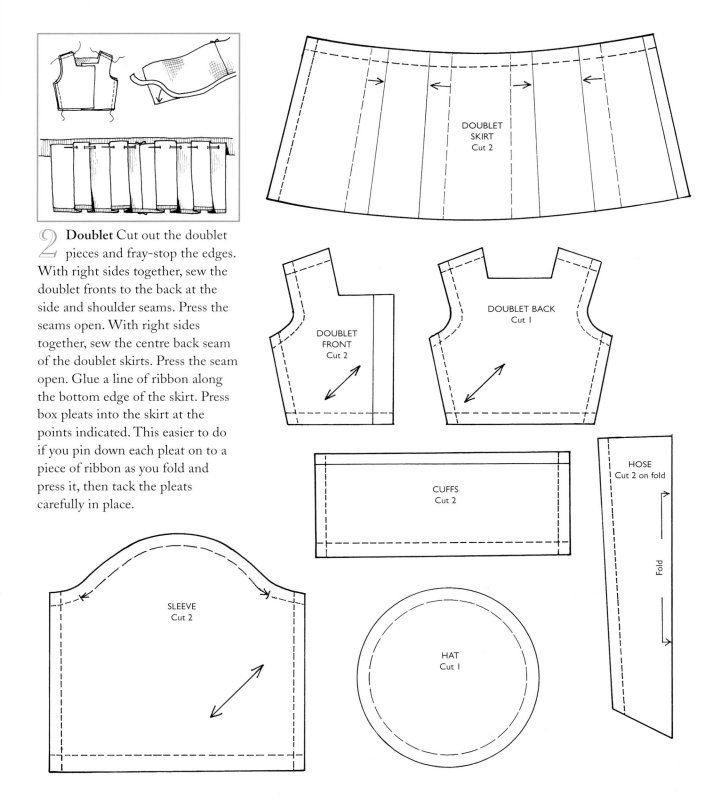

DOUBLET
SKIRT
Cut 2

DOUBLET
FRONT
Cut 2

DOUBLET BACK
Cut 1

CUFFS
Cut 2

HOSE
Cut 2 on fold

Fold

SLEEVE
Cut 2

HAT
Cut 1

2 **Doublet** Cut out the doublet pieces and fray-stop the edges. With right sides together, sew the doublet fronts to the back at the side and shoulder seams. Press the seams open. With right sides together, sew the centre back seam of the doublet skirts. Press the seam open. Glue a line of ribbon along the bottom edge of the skirt. Press box pleats into the skirt at the points indicated. This easier to do if you pin down each pleat on to a piece of ribbon as you fold and press it, then tack the pleats carefully in place.

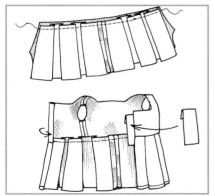

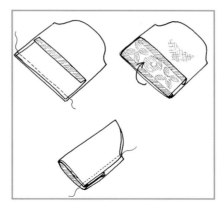

3 **Finishing the doublet** With right sides together, pin the pleated skirt to the bottom of the doublet top, adjusting the pleats to fit. Sew and then press the seam towards the top. Turn back the front edges, pressing them into place with bonding web. Bond or glue a piece of white lawn behind the left front edge to suggest an undershirt. Put the doublet on the doll and pin the two fronts together – they should just meet and have a loose fit.

4 **Sleeves** For each sleeve, press down the sleeve cuff top hem with bonding web. Put the right side of the cuff against the wrong side of the sleeve and sew along the bottom edge to join the cuff to the sleeve along the bottom hem. Turn the cuff over to the right side of the sleeve. With right sides together, sew the sleeve underarm seam, clip and turn.

5 **Finishing** Pull the sleeves on to the doll and ladder stitch to the doublet top, gathering the sleeve top (see page 64). Glue ribbon trim round the neckline and down the fronts, turning the ends over the edge to the back for neatness. Use a stitch or a spot of glue to hold the two fronts together.

6 **Hair and hat** Cut out the hat and run a line of gathering stitches round the gathering line. Pull up to make a beret, tucking the raw edges inside. Wig the man in a Tudor hairstyle (page 123) and glue the hat to his head. Glue a feather to the top of the hat, curling down as shown.

Tudor Girl's Clothes

*Tudor children usually wore similar clothes to their parents
and this little girl has a gown like her mother's. Instead of a headdress, she wears a
simple hairstyle of long flowing hair down her back. You can see the finished Tudor girl
in the photograph on page 77.*

MATERIALS

- Girl doll with Tudor shoes
  (see pages 36–40)
- Patterns for the Tudor girl's clothes
  traced and cut out

Drawers
- Cream cotton lawn

Gown
- Patterned cotton fabric with a
  small stylized print
- Plain contrast silk for the
  sleeve linings
- 2mm (³⁄₃₂in) gold soutache braid

Drawers Cut out the drawers and make as for the woman's drawers on page 68.

Gown Cut out the gown in cotton and the sleeve linings in plain silk. Fray-stop all edges. Make the gown following the instructions on pages 68–9 for the Tudor woman's gown. Glue soutache braid around the neckline and hem.

Hair Wig the doll in the Tudor girl's hairstyle on page 124.

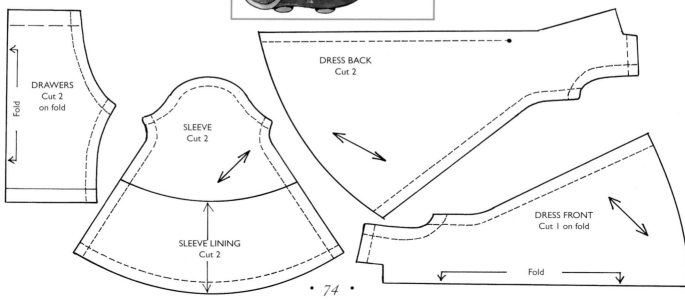

Tudor Boy's Clothes

Young boys of the period were dressed like their adult counterparts and this little boy wears a doublet and hose like his father. Box pleats on such a tiny piece of fabric as the doublet skirt are quite tricky so if you find them very difficult, you can gather the doublet skirt instead. You can see the finished Tudor boy in the photograph on page 77.

MATERIALS

- Boy doll with Tudor shoes (see pages 36–40)
- Patterns for the Tudor boy's clothes traced and cut out

Hose
- Yellow cotton jersey
- 2mm (³/₃₂in) brown soutache braid

Doublet
- Tan silk
- 2mm (³/₃₂in) russet silk ribbon
- 10mm (³/₈in) patterned ribbon or braid for the cuffs

Hose Cut out the hose and follow the Tudor man's hose instructions on page 71. Use the brown soutache to edge the top of the shoes.

Doublet top Cut out the doublet pieces and cut up the centre front of the top. Fray-stop all the edges. Press up a bonded hem on each sleeve. With right sides folded together, sew the side and underarm seams of the doublet top, clip curves and press the seams open.

Doublet skirt Pleat the doublet skirt in the same way as for the Tudor man on pages 72–3. Pin the skirt to the top, right sides together, adjusting the pleats to fit. Sew and press the seam towards the top. Press back 3mm (¹/₈in) down each front edge, using bonding web. Pull on to the doll and slip stitch the fronts together. Glue a line of ribbon down the fronts and round the neck. Glue a cuff of patterned ribbon around the bottom of each sleeve.

Hair Wig the doll with a Tudor fringe and bobbed straight hair as on page 125.

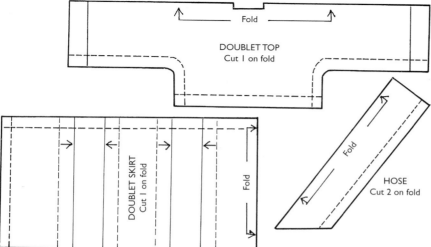

DOUBLET TOP
Cut 1 on fold

DOUBLET SKIRT
Cut 1 on fold

Fold

HOSE
Cut 2 on fold

Tudor Baby's Clothes

Very young babies were tightly swaddled from early times and this was still common practice in the Tudor period. Once they were old enough to be free of swaddling, sixteenth-century paintings show babies wearing simple caps and gowns. Nappies (diapers) were folded rectangles of fabric pinned in place, as they largely continued to be until the twentieth century.

MATERIALS

- Baby doll (see pages 41–3)
- Patterns for the Tudor baby's clothes traced and cut out

Nappy (diaper)
- White voile or lawn

Cap
- White voile or lawn
- 2mm (³/₃₂in) white silk ribbon

Gown
- Cream silk

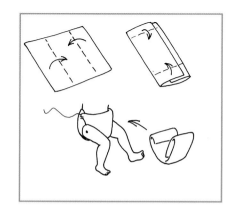

1 **Nappy** Cut out a 60mm (2½in) square of voile for the nappy and fray-stop the edges. Fold the nappy in three lengthways, then fold back the front 20mm (³/₄in) and the back 5mm (³/₁₆in) to make a rectangle. Lay the baby on the nappy and bring the front up between its legs. Stitch the sides to hold.

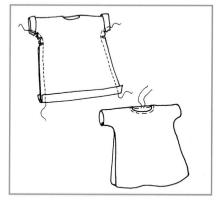

2 **Gown** Cut out the gown and clip the neck opening. Fray-stop all the edges. Press up a bonded hem on each sleeve and along the two bottom edges. Sew the underarm and side seams, clip curves and turn. Run a gathering thread around the neck.

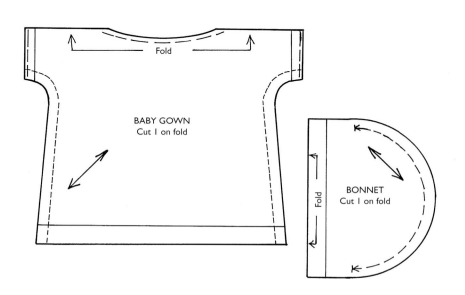

BABY GOWN
Cut 1 on fold

Fold

BONNET
Cut 1 on fold

Fold

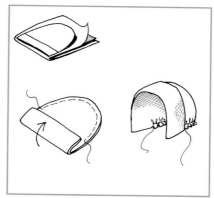

3 **Sleeves** Put the gown on the baby doll, easing the sleeves on to the little bent arms. Pull up the gathers tightly round the neck and stitch to hold. Run tiny gathering stitches around the bottom of each sleeve as close to the folded edge of the hem as possible. Pull up tightly and secure with a stitch or two.

4 **Cap** Fold a small piece of voile in half and bond it together with bonding web. Cut out the cap with the straight edge on the bonded fold. Fray-stop the curved edge. Fold back the straight edge and press into place. Run a gathering thread around the curved edge and pull up to fit the baby's head.

5 **Finishing** Glue a lock of hair on to the front of the baby's head and glue the cap into place over it. Trim the bottom fronts into a curve. Glue a length of ribbon over the raw edge round the back of the cap, covering the gathering stitch. Glue another length of ribbon right round the front of the cap and under the baby's chin. Glue a tiny bow (see page 58) with trailing ends on to the ribbon under the baby's chin.

CHAPTER 8

DRESSING THE DOLLS IN REGENCY COSTUME

The Regency period in Britain in the early nineteenth century produced a return to simplicity and taste after the excesses of Georgian fashion, while a similar revolution occurred in North America at the same time. This is a popular period for miniaturists – architecture, interior design and clothing all reflected the contemporary enthusiasm for Roman and Greek classical style. Clothes of this period are often referred to as 'Empire style'. In the photograph, a Regency family is visiting friends. All the clothes are either projects in this chapter or variations of the patterns using different fabrics and trims.

FABRICS

In summer, women wore white or pastel dresses in muslin and poplin and decoration was often small sprig patterns or touches of colour in the embroidery and trimmings. Winter fashions tended to be of bolder colours in silks and wool in colours such as the amethyst, ruby and amber listed in a women's magazine of the period. Men wore light-coloured breeches, light waistcoats and dark tailcoats of black, dark blue, burgundy or green.

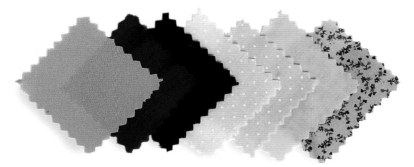

Regency Woman's Clothes

This is the type of clothing worn by Jane Austen's heroines: a high-waisted dress in white or pastel colours with short puff sleeves. Women at this time usually wore only petticoats and flesh-coloured stockings under their clothes. If you wish to dress your doll in drawers, use the Victorian pattern for these on pages 92–3 but leave the legs ungathered.

MATERIALS

- Woman doll with all-in-one arms and Regency shoes (see pages 19–26)
- Patterns for the Regency woman's clothes traced and cut out

Dress
- White fine cotton or voile with a small print or spot
- 2mm (³⁄₃₂in) pink silk ribbon

Bonnet
- Cream silk
- Interlining
- 2mm (³⁄₃₂in) cream soutache braid
- 2mm (³⁄₃₂in) cream silk ribbon

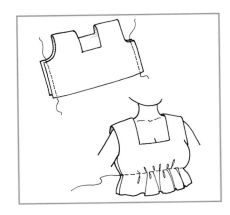

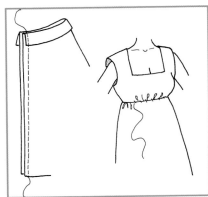

1 **Bodice** Cut out the dress pieces and fray-stop the edges. With right sides together, sew the side seams of the bodice, press and turn. Pull the bodice on to the doll. You will have to push her arms above her head in order to do this. Run a gathering thread along the line under the bust and right round the back. Pull up to gather, arranging the gathers under the bust and across the back.

2 **Skirt** Press under 6mm (¼in) along the top edge of the skirt. With right sides together, sew the back seam. Press the seam open and turn. Pull on to the doll and check the length, trimming if necessary. The skirt is attached over the bottom of the bodice. Slip stitch it in place just above the line of gathering on the bodice, gathering the sides of the skirt slightly as you sew.

BONNET
BACK

BONNET BRIM

SLEEVE
Cut 2

Back

BODICE
Cut I

Front

SKIRT
Cut I on fold

Fold

VARIATIONS

The grandmother on page 79 wears a variation of this costume. The long sleeves are made by gluing a length of matching fabric around each arm and then covering it with the puff sleeves.

The neck is filled in with a gathered length of lace. Her mob-cap is made in white lawn using the Tudor man's hat pattern, and edged with narrow lace.

3 **Sleeves** Sew a gathering stitch along the top and bottom edge of the sleeves. Sew the sleeve seams. Pull a sleeve on to the doll, bottom edge first and still inside out. Draw up the gathers tightly to fit, tie off, then pull the sleeve up on to the shoulder.

4 **Finishing** Pull up the gathers on the top of the sleeve and ladder stitch to the bodice (see page 64). Repeat for the second sleeve. Glue ribbon all round the bottom hem, neckline and waist of the dress.

Hair Wig the doll in the Regency woman's style (see page 121). If the doll is to wear a bonnet, omit the bun.

6 **Decoration** Fit the bonnet on to the doll. Glue ribbon to one side of the bonnet, round under the chin and to the other side. Glue ribbon rosettes (see page 58) to cover the ends of the ribbon. Tie a bow (see page 58) and glue in place under the chin.

5 **Bonnet** Double bond a small piece of silk by folding it in half, inserting a piece of bonding web and ironing the two pieces together. Cut out the bonnet brim and back from this. Fold back the tabs on the bonnet back and glue the brim over them. Glue soutache braid round the brim and gather some more soutache (by pulling a side thread) to trim the back.

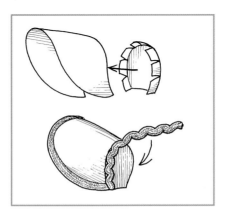

Regency Man's Clothes

This is a typical outfit for a man of the period. He has a tailcoat, waistcoat, breeches and a white cravat tied in the 'Byron' style popular at the time. It was fashionable to wear a tailcoat open and the waistcoat was always slightly longer than the front of the coat.

MATERIALS

- Man doll with Regency shoes
  (see pages 27–33)
- Patterns for the Regency man's
  clothes traced and cut out
  (see page 84)

Breeches
- Beige or cream cotton

Shirt
- White lawn
- Interlining

Cravat
- Fine white silk

Waistcoat
- White or cream silk
- Small white polymer clay buttons
  (see page 58)

Tailcoat
- Sage green silk
- Gold polymer clay buttons
  (see page 58)

Top hat
- Thin card
- Black acrylic paint
- 2mm (3/32in) black silk ribbon

1 Breeches Cut out the breeches and fray-stop the edges. Turn under the hem on the leg bottoms and press. With right sides together, sew the front and back body seams. Clip curves, press and fold again as shown. Sew the inside leg seam, clip curves and press.

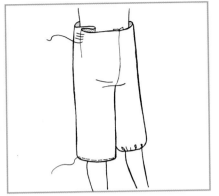

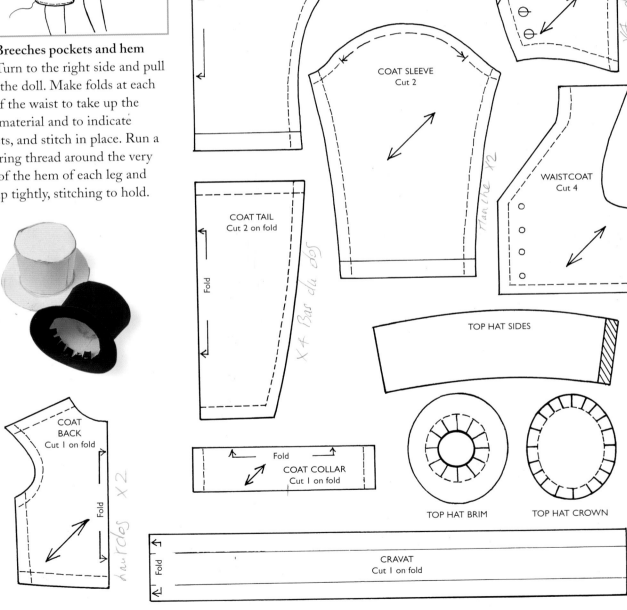

2 **Breeches pockets and hem**
Turn to the right side and pull on to the doll. Make folds at each side of the waist to take up the extra material and to indicate pockets, and stitch in place. Run a gathering thread around the very edge of the hem of each leg and pull up tightly, stitching to hold.

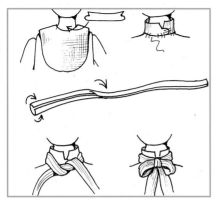

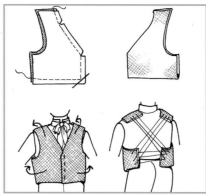

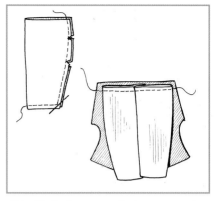

3 **Shirt** Cut out the shirt front and glue lightly to the doll's chest. Iron bonded interlining on to a small piece of lawn and cut out the collar on the cross. Check for size, trimming to fit, and place round the neck. Stitch the overlap together and use a few stitches to hold the collar in place on the shirt front.

Cravat Cut out the cravat and press the long edges to the centre, then press in half lengthways. Tie tightly round the collar and finish with a bow. Stitch the ends to the shirt front to hold them down and trim off the excess.

4 **Waistcoat** The back is omitted to avoid bulk. Cut out the pieces and fray-stop the edges. With right sides together, sew each front and facing together along the front and bottom edges, turning the corners neatly. Clip curves and corners, turn and press thoroughly. Sew the two fronts together along the button line, overlapping left over right (see page 65). Place on the doll's front over the top of the trousers and use tacking stitches across the back to hold the waistcoat in place. Slip stitch the bottom of the waistcoat to the trousers at the sides to hold them together.

5 **Tails** Cut out all the coat pieces and fray-stop the edges. Fold each tail piece right sides together and sew the side and bottom seams. Clip, turn and press. With right sides together, sew the tail pieces to the bottom of the coat back, overlapping them in the centre. The curved sides of the tails should face outwards and the top edges should be placed 3mm ($\frac{1}{8}$in) in from the coat back sides. Press the seam allowance upwards.

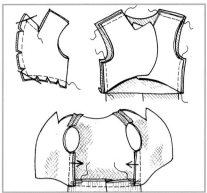

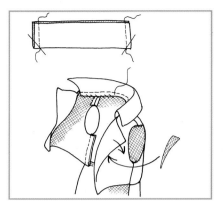

6 **Coat** With right sides together, sew the fronts to the front facings along the front and bottom edges; stitch round the corners neatly so they will make good points. Clip the curves and corners and turn, pushing out the points from the inside with a blunt needle. Press firmly. With right sides together, sew the fronts to the back at the side and shoulder seams. Press the seam allowances towards the back and slip stitch the side seam allowance to the back of the coat.

7 **Lapels** Press the lapels down firmly, using bonding web to hold them in place.

Collar Fold the collar in half lengthways with right sides together and sew the end seams. Clip the corners, turn and press. Sew the collar to the inside back of the coat top, then slip stitch the raw edge in place to hold it down. Press the collar down using a strip of bonding web or a few stitches to hold it in place on the coat back.

9 **Hair** Wig the doll in the Regency men's style (see page 123). If he is to wear a top hat, keep the crown hair thin.

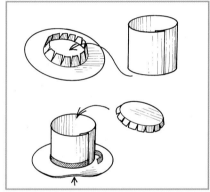

8 **Sleeves** Turn under a hem on each sleeve using bonding web. The sleeves should come down low over the hands. Sew the sleeve seams, clip and turn. Place the coat on the doll and pin the front closed. Ladder stitch each sleeve to the armhole (see page 64), gathering it slightly at the shoulder.

Buttons Glue buttons to the right front of the coat and make corresponding horizontal stitches to suggest buttonholes on the left front. Glue the buttons to the front of the waistcoat.

10 **Top hat** Cut out the hat pieces in card. Score firmly along the dashed fold lines and push the tabs up on the brim, down on the top. Glue the hat sides into a cylinder, overlapping the shaded area, and apply glue around the inside of the bottom. Fit over the tabs on the brim, pushing them on to the glue from below. Repeat for the tabs on the hat top. Paint the hat thickly with black acrylic paint. Bend the brim up slightly on the long sides and glue a piece of narrow ribbon round the hat.

Regency Girl's Clothes

Little girls at this time wore similar high-waisted dresses to their mothers, often in white muslin with a pastel sash. Short, curly hairstyles were popular and in keeping with the classical theme of the period. Use the Victorian pattern for the drawers and leave the legs ungathered.

MATERIALS

- Girl doll with Regency shoes (see pages 36–40)
- Patterns for Regency girl's clothes traced and cut out

Drawers
- White lawn

Dress
- White lawn
- 2mm ($^3/_{32}$in) lilac silk ribbon
- 6mm ($^1/_4$in) white lace

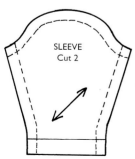

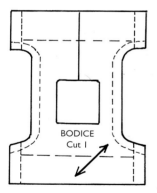

BODICE
Cut 1

Drawers Cut out the drawers and make as for the woman's drawers on page 92, leaving the legs ungathered.

Dress Cut out the dress pieces and fray-stop all edges. With right sides

together, sew the bodice side seams, turn, press and pull on to the doll. Fold over one side and slip stitch the backs together, adjusting to fit. Run a gathering thread around the bodice and draw up. Make the skirt following the instructions for the woman's skirt on page 80 and slip stitch it to the bodice. If the neck gapes, run a gathering thread along the neck front and gather slightly.

Sleeves Hem the bottom of the sleeves using bonding web and sew the sleeve seams, leaving the bottom 6mm ($^1/_4$in) unsewn so you can pull them over the doll's hands. Clip curves and turn. Pull each sleeve on to the doll and ladder stitch to the bodice (see page 64). Slip stitch the cuffs together. Glue lace around the hem and cuffs. Trim around the neck with a narrow strip cut from the lace, covering the raw edges and gathers. Glue a sash of ribbon round the waist with a bow at the back.

Hair Wig the doll with a simple short, curly hairstyle (see page 124).

Shoes Glue rosettes of ribbon to the shoe fronts (see page 58).

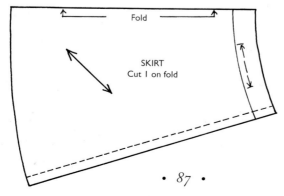

SLEEVE
Cut 2

Fold

SKIRT
Cut 1 on fold

Regency Boy's Clothes

*The rather oddly named skeleton suit became fashionable for little boys
at the end of the eighteenth century and remained popular for many years.
The trousers are high-waisted and buttoned to the jacket, which is
worn over a shirt with a frilly collar.*

MATERIALS

- Boy doll with Regency shoes
  (see pages 36–40)
- Patterns for Regency boy's clothes
  traced and cut out

Jacket
- Light blue cotton fabric
- 6mm (¼in) white lace
- 13 light blue polymer clay buttons
  (see page 58)

Trousers
- White or cream silk

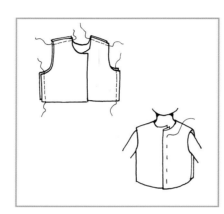

1 Jacket top Cut out the jacket pieces and fray-stop all edges. With right sides together, sew the jacket fronts to the back at the side and shoulder seams. Turn and press. Pull on to the doll, fold under the allowance on the left front and stitch in place over the right front (see page 65).

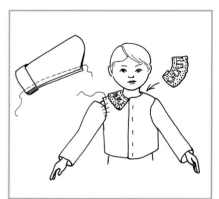

2 Sleeves Hem the bottom of the sleeves using bonding web and sew the sleeve seams. Clip and turn. Pull each sleeve on to the doll and ladder stitch in place (see page 64). Fold under the end of a piece of lace and glue to the neckline and over one shoulder, repeating for the other side to make a collar. You can glue a third piece to the back of the neck to neaten it if necessary.

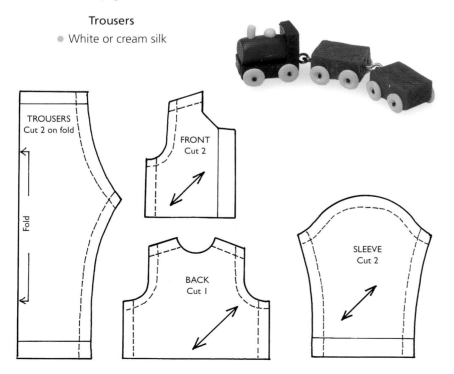

TROUSERS
Cut 2 on fold

Fold

FRONT
Cut 2

BACK
Cut 1

SLEEVE
Cut 2

3 **Trousers** Cut out the trouser pieces and fray-stop the edges. Use bonding web to press under 3mm (⅛in) along the top edges and, after checking for length, the hems. The top of the trousers need to come fairly high up the jacket. Sew the front and back body seams, clip curves, then sew the inside leg seam. Clip curves and turn.

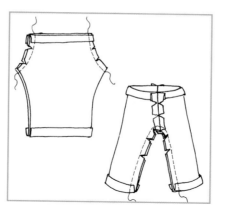

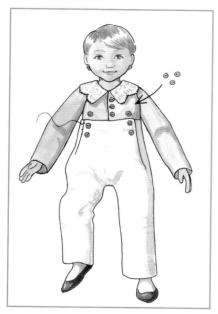

4 **Finishing** Pull the trousers on to the doll over the bottom of the jacket and take up the extra fabric by making a pleat on either side of the centre front and slip stitching in place all round the high waistline. Glue buttons to the jacket and trouser fronts as shown.

Hair Wig the boy doll with short hair, either straight or curly (see page 125).

THE BABY'S CLOTHES

Baby wear changes remarkably little over the centuries. For a Regency baby, use the instructions for the Victorian baby on page 99. Cut the gown shorter and use narrower lace on the bonnet as Regency preferences were for simpler clothes.

CHAPTER 9

DRESSING THE DOLLS
IN VICTORIAN COSTUME

Fashions during the long reign of Queen Victoria in the nineteenth century varied considerably. The clothes in this chapter are typical of the middle of the century when the full-skirted crinoline was at its most popular and men wore frock coats. In the photograph, a Victorian family takes tea in the drawing room. All the family's clothes are either projects in this chapter or variations of the patterns using different fabric and trims. Further examples are shown on page 98.

FABRICS

Women wore soft, light colours in cotton and silk for spring and summer. Winter wear was of more sombre colours in wool and taffeta. Patterned fabrics were popular, especially small florals and tartans. Men's frock coats were usually black and worn with a tastefully patterned or plain waistcoat and a cravat. Trousers were light or dark and sometimes checked or in the fabric of the coat.

Victorian Woman's Clothes

The doll in the photograph wears a flounced tartan dress with full sleeves over drawers trimmed with lace. A second pattern for the skirt is given without the flounces for a plainer style and you can make the dress in a variety of fabrics; coloured silk with ribbon trim looks very pretty.

MATERIALS

- Woman doll with Victorian boots (see pages 19–26)
- Patterns for the Victorian woman's clothes traced and cut out

Drawers
- White lawn
- 6mm (¼in) white lace

Dress
- Cotton miniature tartan fabric
- 6mm (¼in) white lace
- 2mm (³⁄₃₂in) navy silk ribbon
- Matching polymer clay buttons (see page 58)

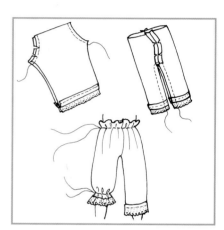

1 **Drawers** Cut out the drawers, press up the hem on the leg bottoms and sew a length of lace along each. Place the right sides together and sew the front and back body seams. Clip curves, press and then sew the inside leg seam. Clip curves and press. Turn to the right side and pull on to the doll. Run a gathering thread around the waist, pull up tightly and tie off. Leave the drawers legs straight or gather in the same way as the waist.

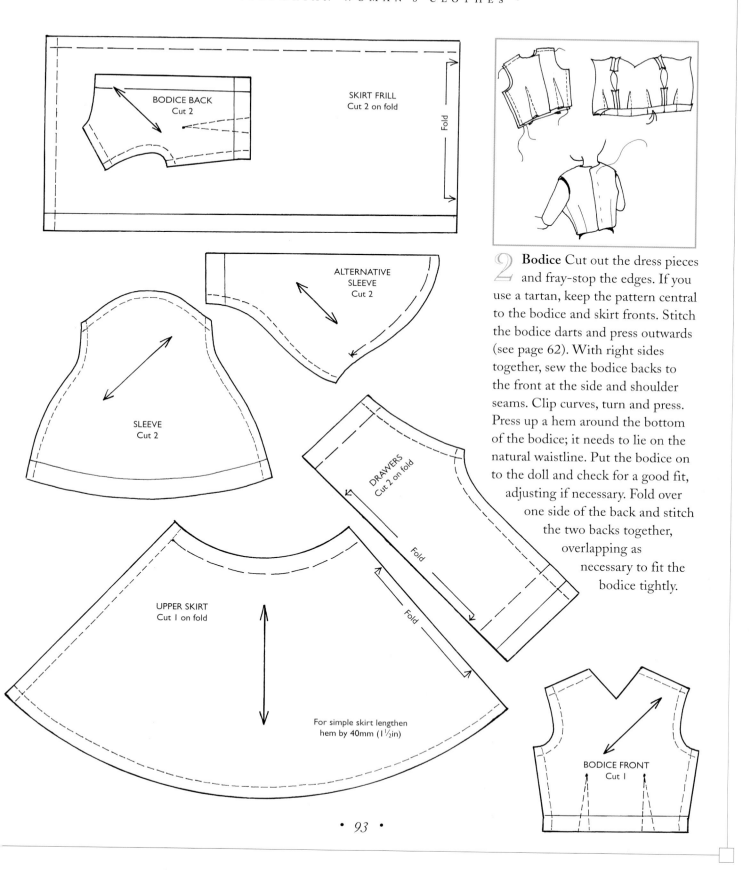

BODICE BACK
Cut 2

SKIRT FRILL
Cut 2 on fold

Fold

ALTERNATIVE
SLEEVE
Cut 2

SLEEVE
Cut 2

DRAWERS
Cut 2 on fold

Fold

Fold

UPPER SKIRT
Cut 1 on fold

For simple skirt lengthen
hem by 40mm (1½in)

BODICE FRONT
Cut 1

Bodice Cut out the dress pieces and fray-stop the edges. If you use a tartan, keep the pattern central to the bodice and skirt fronts. Stitch the bodice darts and press outwards (see page 62). With right sides together, sew the bodice backs to the front at the side and shoulder seams. Clip curves, turn and press. Press up a hem around the bottom of the bodice; it needs to lie on the natural waistline. Put the bodice on to the doll and check for a good fit, adjusting if necessary. Fold over one side of the back and stitch the two backs together, overlapping as necessary to fit the bodice tightly.

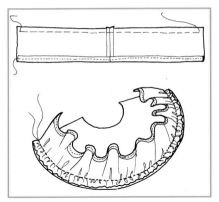

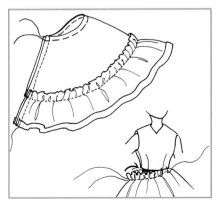

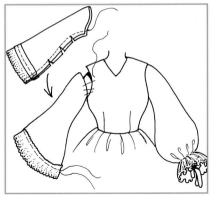

3 **Skirt frill** With right sides together, sew the two frill pieces together into one length and press the seam open. Turn up and sew a single hem on the bottom of the frill. Run a gathering stitch along the top edge and pull up to fit the bottom of the upper skirt. With right sides together, pin and sew to the upper skirt. Press the seam allowance upwards.

4 **Skirt** Run a gathering stitch around the top of the skirt and, with right sides together, sew the central back seam. Press the seam open and turn. Pull the skirt on to the doll and pull up the gathers, tying off tightly. Slip stitch the bodice bottom edge to the skirt gathering line, covering the raw edges and gathering stitches.

5 **Sleeves** Cut out the sleeves and fray-stop the edges. Press up a hem along each bottom edge and sew on a length of lace. Sew the underarm seams, clip the curves and turn. Pull each sleeve on to the doll and ladder stitch to the armhole (see page 64). Run a gathering thread around the wrist, at the top of the lace, pull up and tie off tightly. The sleeve should bell out over the wrist.

6 **Finishing** Trim the neckline if necessary and glue on a snippet of lace for the collar. Glue or stitch ribbon along the top of the frill and around the waist to cover any stitching. Glue buttons to the back of the dress.

Hair Wig the doll in the Victorian hairstyle on page 121. If you wish to make a bonnet, use the instructions on page 82 for the Regency bonnet but trim the bonnet more lavishly with roses, ribbons or feathers.

VARIATIONS

A second pattern for a different style of sleeves, which are full at the shoulders, is provided on page 93 as well as the simple skirt pattern. On page 98, the doll in the brown dress is costumed using these patterns, which are made up in the same way on the bodice. The grandmother is dressed in a simple skirt with the first style of sleeves and wears a bonnet. With this combination of patterns you can make many different dresses for your Victorian dolls.

Victorian Man's Clothes

*The doll in the photograph is dressed in typical clothes of the Victorian era.
Men's clothes did not vary a great deal at this time and this outfit, with only minor
variations, would be suitable for the period between about 1830 and 1900. Plain silk trousers
and a silk waistcoat are worn with a stiff-collared shirt, a cravat and a frock coat.*

MATERIALS

Man doll with black boots
(see pages 27–33)
Patterns for the Victorian man's clothes
traced and cut out
(see page 96)

Trousers
- Fine light grey silk.

Waistcoat
- Gold silk or a fine printed cotton
- 4 gold polymer clay buttons
(see page 58)

Shirt
- White lawn
- Interlining

Cravat
- Very thin blue silk

Frock coat
- Black cotton fabric
- 4 black polymer clay buttons
(see page 58)

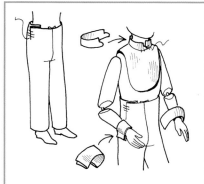

1 **Trousers** Cut out the trousers and fray-stop the edges. Turn up the bottom hems with bonding web. Make and fit the trousers as for the Regency man on pages 83–4 but do not gather the bottom hems.

Shirt Make up the collar and shirt front as for the Regency man on page 85. Fold a piece of lawn in half and iron together with bonding web. Cut out the cuffs with one long edge of each on the fold. Stitch the cuffs in place at the wrists with the folded edge to the front.

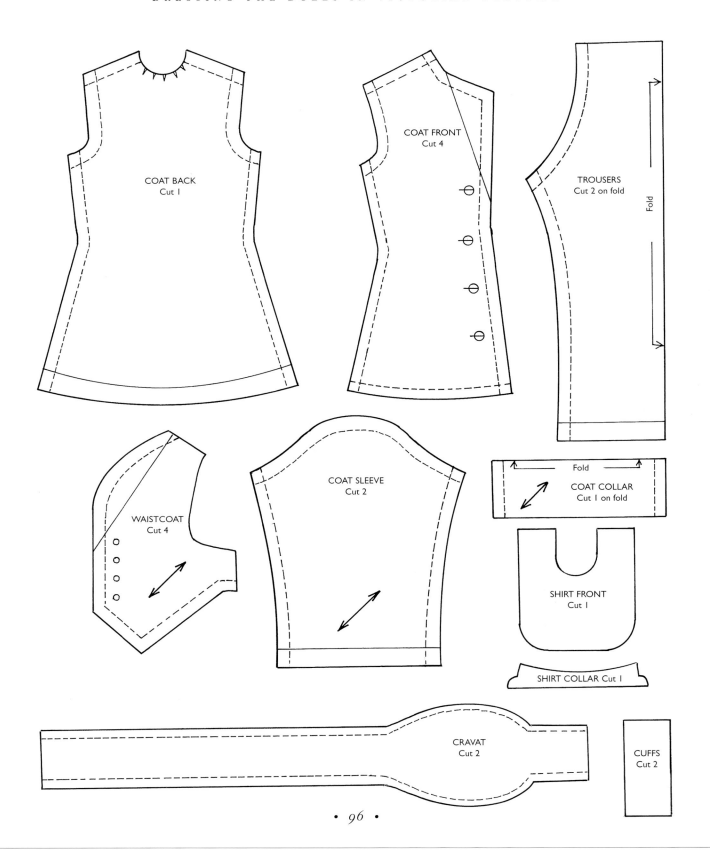

COAT BACK
Cut 1

COAT FRONT
Cut 4

TROUSERS
Cut 2 on fold

Fold

Fold

COAT COLLAR
Cut 1 on fold

WAISTCOAT
Cut 4

COAT SLEEVE
Cut 2

SHIRT FRONT
Cut 1

SHIRT COLLAR Cut 1

CRAVAT
Cut 2

CUFFS
Cut 2

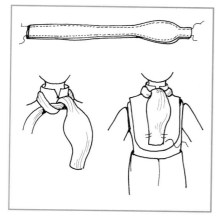

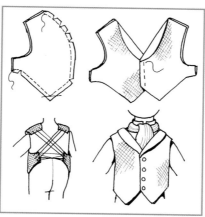

2 **Cravat** Cut out the cravat and with right sides together, sew the two pieces together. Turn using a safety pin (see page 63) and press. Wrap round the neck and tie in a simple knot with the wide part to the front. Use a stitch of thread to hold it on to the shirt front and trim the ends if necessary.

3 **Waistcoat** Cut out the waistcoat and fray-stop the edges. With right sides together, sew the fronts to the facings along the front and bottom edges, taking care to turn the corners neatly. Clip curves and corners, turn and press. Press the lapels back and hold in place with slip stitches or bonding web. Place the two fronts together, overlapping left over right, and stitch together along the button line (see page 65). Fit the waistcoat on to the doll and hold in place with tacking stitches across the back.

4 **Frock coat** Cut out all the pieces and fray-stop the edges. With right sides together, sew the fronts to the front facings along the front and bottom edges. Clip the curves and corners, turn and press firmly. With right sides together, sew the fronts to the back at the side and shoulder seams. Clip curves and press the shoulder seams open and the side seams towards the back. Try the coat on the doll and check for fit. Turn up the bottom hem of the coat back, covering the bottom of the side seam allowance, and press into place with bonding web.

5 **Collar** Sew the collar side seams, clip the corners, turn and press firmly. Sew the collar to the inside of the coat top, aligning centres and clipping the coat neck on the back to ease the fit. You may need to apply more fray-stop here to prevent fraying. Press down the collar and lapels using bonding web or slip stitch to hold them in place.

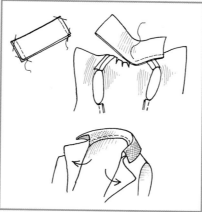

6 **Sleeves** Turn up a hem on each sleeve using bonding web. Sew the sleeve seams, clip curves and turn. With the coat on the doll, pin the fronts together, and slide the sleeves on to the arms. Ladder stitch the sleeves to the armholes (see page 64).

7 **Buttons** Glue buttons to the right coat front and make corresponding horizontal stitches on the left front for buttonholes. Glue the buttons to the waistcoat.

Hair Wig the doll with the Victorian man's hairstyle (see page 124). Most Victorian men wore a top hat and the instructions for this are on page 86.

VARIATIONS

These dolls show variations on the adult patterns. The maid's dress is made from the woman's patterns with a simple apron added. Her cap is a scrap of lace with a ribbon bow on top and the ends of ribbon left long. The butler wears black Victorian trousers and a black Regency tailcoat; typical wear for a butler. See page 94 for a description of the grandmothers and younger woman's clothes.

Victorian Baby's Clothes

The Victorians dressed their babies in copious quantities of frills and exceptionally long baby gowns decorated with lace and embroidery. This little baby has a frilly bonnet and a long lacy gown that you can dress up with more lace if you wish.

1. **Nappy** Use the instructions for the Tudor baby's nappy on page 76.

2. **Gown** Make the gown as for the Tudor baby's gown on page 76, cutting the gown pattern 35mm (1³⁄₈in) longer. Stitch the lace all round the bottom of the baby's gown.

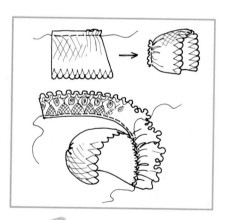

3. **Bonnet** Cut a piece of the wide lace 40mm (1¹⁄₂in) long. Run a gathering thread along one long side and pull up to make the back of the bonnet, stitching to secure. Cut a 75mm (3in) length of the narrow lace and run a gathering thread along one long side. Pull up until it fits the front edge of the bonnet back. Slip stitch the gathered edge to the front edge of the bonnet back, finishing the ends neatly.

4. **Hair** Wig the baby with tiny curls of hair all over the head (see page 125). Pull the bonnet on to the head. Stitch a piece of ribbon to each side of the bonnet, passing under the baby's chin. Make a bow and fix under the chin (see page 58).

MATERIALS

● Baby doll
(see pages 41–3)
● Patterns for Tudor baby's gown lengthened, traced and cut out
(see page 76)

Nappy (diaper)
● White voile or lawn

Gown
● White silk jacquard
● 20mm (³⁄₄in) fine white lace

Bonnet
● 20mm (³⁄₄in) white lace
● 13mm (¹⁄₂in) white edging lace

Victorian Girl's Clothes

This little girl wears a full-skirted dress in pink silk with her lacy drawers showing beneath in typical Victorian style. Queen Victoria often sketched her children and the dress is adapted from one of her watercolours.

MATERIALS

- Girl doll with Victorian boots (see pages 36–40)
- Patterns for Victorian girl's clothes traced and cut out

Drawers
- White lawn
- 6mm (¼in) white lace

Dress
- Fine pink silk
- 2mm (³⁄₃₂in) silk ribbon in light and dark pink
- 6mm (¼in) white lace

1 Drawers Cut out the drawers and follow the instructions for the women's drawers on page 92.

Skirt Cut out the skirt and fray-stop the edges. Sew a gathering thread along the top edge. Sew the centre back seam and press open. Glue the two colours of ribbon along the bottom of the skirt, using glue very sparingly on the silk. Pull on to the doll and pull up the gathers to fit the waist, tying off tightly. The drawers should show below the skirt.

VARIATIONS

Boots were normal footwear for Victorian children but for a daintier effect, you could make the doll with simple black shoes and white stockings. These can be with or without ankle straps (see page 39) and were sometimes worn for a party or special occasion.

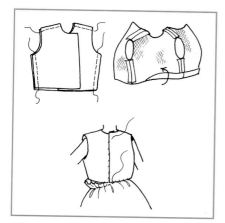

2 **Bodice** Cut out the bodice and fray-stop the edges. With right sides together, sew the backs to the front at the side and shoulder seams. Turn, press and try on the doll – you need a fairly tight fit so adjust the pattern at this point if necessary. Press up a hem all round the bottom edge so that the folded edge lies on the natural waistline. Fold one bodice back over the other and slip stitch in place. Slip stitch the bottom edge of the bodice to the skirt.

3 **Sleeves** Cut out the sleeves and fray-stop the edges. Sew the underarm seams, clip curves and turn. Pull each sleeve on to the doll and ladder stitch to the bodice (see page 64). Run a gathering thread around each wrist, pull up and secure with a few stitches. Glue a scrap of lace round the raw edges of each wrist.

Trim the bodice by lightly gluing on ribbon in a point as shown. Glue a bow to the front of the waist (see page 58). Glue small sections cut from lace around the neck, covering the raw edges.

Hair Wig the doll in the Victorian girl's hairstyle on page 125. Use matching ribbons for bows and glue them above the ringlets.

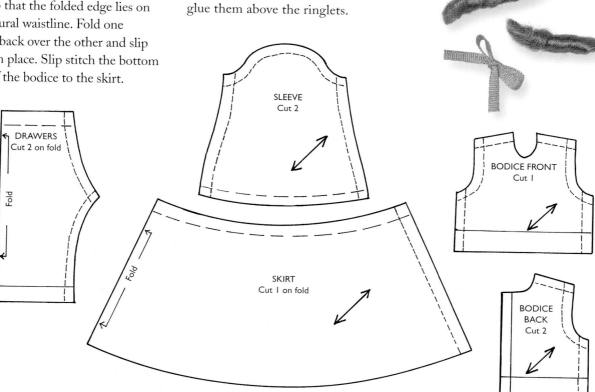

DRAWERS
Cut 2 on fold

Fold

SLEEVE
Cut 2

SKIRT
Cut 1 on fold

Fold

BODICE FRONT
Cut 1

BODICE
BACK
Cut 2

Victorian Boy's Clothes

Victorians dressed little boys in frocks and frills until they were 'breeched' at about six years old – meaning that they were allowed to wear trousers for the first time. A popular first suit was the knickerbocker suit which is shown here; knickerbocker trousers were worn with a short jacket over a shirt with a lacy collar.

MATERIALS

- Boy doll Victorian boots (see pages 36–40)
- Patterns for Victorian boy's clothes traced and cut out

Suit
- Light brown cotton fabric
- 6mm (¼in) white lace for the collar
- 4 brown polymer clay buttons (see page 58)

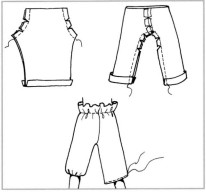

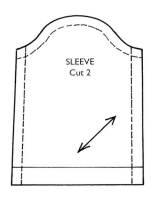

SLEEVE Cut 2

1 Knickerbockers Cut out the knickerbockers and fray-stop the edges. Press up the hem on each leg. With right sides together, sew the front and back body seams. Clip curves, press, then sew the inside leg seam. Clip curves and turn. Pull the trousers on to the doll. Run a gathering thread around the folded edge of each leg bottom, pull up and tie off tightly just below the knee. The knickerbockers should bell over the gathering. Run a gathering thread around the waist, pull up and tie off.

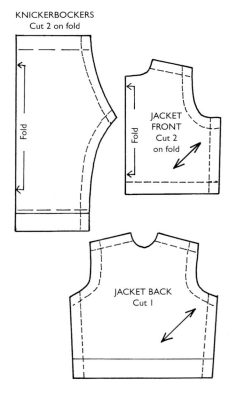

KNICKERBOCKERS Cut 2 on fold

Fold

Fold

JACKET FRONT Cut 2 on fold

JACKET BACK Cut 1

2 **Jacket** Cut out the jacket pieces and fray-stop the edges. With right sides together, sew the bottom edge of each jacket front. Clip the corners, turn and press. With right sides together, sew the fronts to the jacket back at the sides and shoulder seams. Turn and press the side seams towards the back. Press up the bottom hem allowance on the back, covering the bottoms of the side seam allowances, and use bonding web to hold.

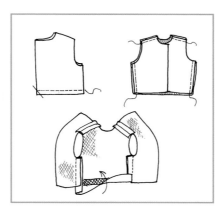

3 **Finishing** Put the jacket on to the doll and stitch the fronts together with a slight overlap (see page 64).

Sleeves Use bonding web to turn up the sleeve hems. Sew the underarm seams, clip curves and turn. Pull each sleeve on to the doll and ladder stitch to the jacket (see page 64).

Collar Glue two pieces of lace on to the neck to form a lacy collar and glue four brown buttons to the jacket front.

Hair Wig the doll in a boy's straight or curly hairstyle (see page 125).

CHAPTER 10

DRESSING THE DOLLS IN EDWARDIAN COSTUME

The early twentieth century was a time of elegance and good taste in fashion. Women's clothes had a slimmer line with big hats, puffy blouses and tight waists. Men's clothes became more varied with the appearance of different jackets and blazers for informal wear. In the photograph, an Edwardian Mama and Papa have brought their children to visit their grandmother. All the clothes are either projects in this chapter or variations of the patterns using different fabric and trims.

FABRICS

A greater variety of fabrics became available at the turn of the twentieth century and women's clothes were made in crêpe de chine, voile, poplin, silks and piqué – to name just a few popular materials. Very sheer fabrics such as chiffon and muslin were worn in summer, while wool, cashmere, tweed and velour were popular for winter wear. Women's clothes were usually made in pastel colours for the summer with darker fabrics used in winter. Men still wore wool for their jackets and coats, and while sombre colours were still favoured, lighter colours were now used for some summer wear.

Edwardian Woman's Clothes

This doll is wearing a typical Edwardian blouse in white voile with a pouched front and puffed sleeves while her camisole is just visible through the sheer fabric. Her skirt has five panels and is slightly longer at the back. If you wish to give the doll drawers, use the pattern for the Victorian doll.

MATERIALS

- Woman doll with Edwardian boots (see pages 19–26)
- Patterns for the Edwardian woman's clothes traced and cut out

Camisole
- 25mm (1in) white lace

Blouse
- White cotton voile
- 13mm (½in) white lace

Skirt
- Lilac silk
- Matching 6mm (¼in) ribbon
- 6mm (¼in) patterned or plain ribbon

Hat
- Cream silk
- Interlining
- 2mm (³/₃₂in) cream soutache braid
- 5mm (³/₈in) organdie ribbon in white and pink
- Scraps of pale green silk ribbon
- 25mm (1in) white lace

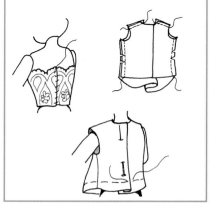

1 **Camisole** Cut a length of the 25mm (1in) lace long enough to go around the doll's bust. Wrap the lace round the doll just below the arms and covering the bust. Stitch in place up the back.

Blouse Cut out the blouse pieces and fray-stop all the edges. With right sides together, sew the backs to the front at the side and shoulder seams. Clip curves and press the seams open. Turn and put on to the doll. Fold one side of the back over the other and pin in place.

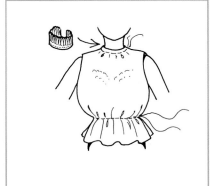

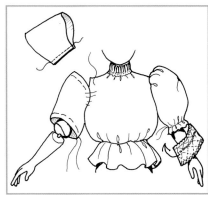

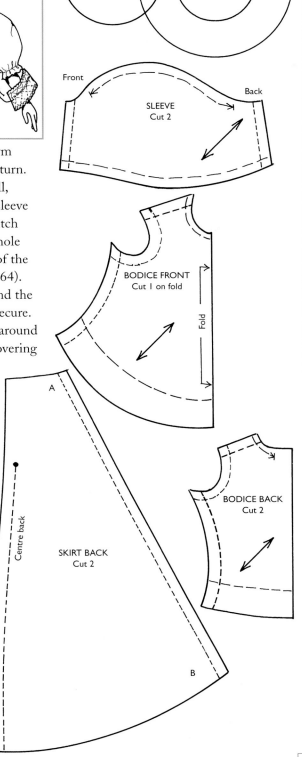

HAT CROWN

HAT BRIM

Front

Back

SLEEVE
Cut 2

2 Gathering the blouse Run a gathering thread all round the blouse along the marked gathering line. Pull up to gather to the waist, arranging the gathers so that the front of the blouse pouches over. Slip stitch the back closure. Run a gathering thread around the neck and pull up to gather the neck slightly. Glue a strip of lace around the neck as an upstanding collar, covering the raw edges.

3 Sleeves Sew the underarm seam of each sleeve and turn. Pull each sleeve on to the doll, ensuring the full part of the sleeve top is to the front. Ladder stitch the sleeves neatly to the armhole openings, gathering the top of the sleeve as you do so (see page 64). Run a gathering thread around the sleeve bottoms, pull up and secure. Glue a length of lace tightly around each arm below the sleeve, covering the gathered raw edge.

BODICE FRONT
Cut 1 on fold

Fold

BODICE BACK
Cut 2

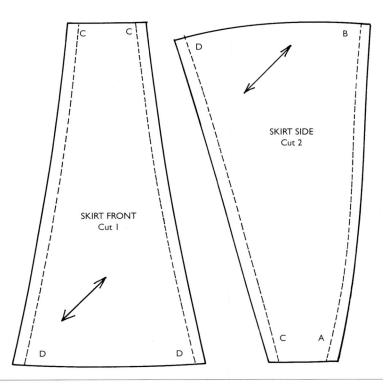

SKIRT FRONT
Cut 1

SKIRT SIDE
Cut 2

A

Centre back

SKIRT BACK
Cut 2

B

C

D

C

C

D

B

D

D

C

A

4 **Skirt** Cut out the skirt panels and fray-stop the edges. With right sides together, sew all the side seams, matching the letters and sewing as accurately as possible to ensure a good fit. Clip curves and press the seams open. Sew the centre back seam to the dot. Try on the doll and check the length, trimming if necessary – the skirt should just cover the feet and trail behind a little. Stitch or glue a line of ribbon trim to the bottom hem.

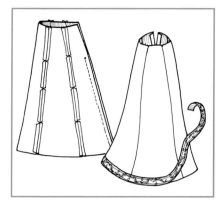

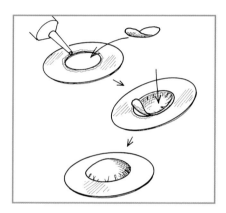

5 **Waistband** Put the skirt on to the doll and slip stitch the centre back edges together, pulling the skirt tight around the hips. Glue a piece of matching ribbon around the waist, covering the raw top edge and pulling it tight. The blouse should bell over the top of the waistband.

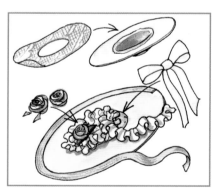

Hair Wig the doll in the Edwardian woman's hairstyle (see page 121). The hat should fit over the hair and you can use a pin or two to hold it in place, just as real hat pins were worn!

6 **Hat** Iron a small piece of interlining on to a piece of silk and cut out the hat brim. Cut out the hat crown in unlined silk and fray-stop the edge. Apply a thin line of glue around the inner edge of the brim on its underside (the side with the interlining). Press the edge of the crown piece on to this all round, easing it into the hole to make it fit and so doming the silk through the hole to make a simple crown.

7 **Trimmings** Cut out a lining for the hat brim in the lace and glue on under the brim, covering the raw edges of the crown. Glue soutache braid around the top edge of the brim. Make a ruffle trim with organdie ribbon (see page 58) and glue all over the crown. Make three ribbon roses in pink organdie ribbon (see page 59) and glue in amongst the white with snippets of green ribbon to suggest leaves. Make a large bow in the white organdie ribbon (see page 58) and glue on the top back of the crown.

Edwardian Man's Clothes

The man doll is wearing a slate grey lounge jacket, black trousers and a patterned waistcoat. He wears a boater and carries a cane made from a bamboo barbecue skewer topped with a ball of painted clay.

MATERIALS

- Man doll with Edwardian shoes or boots (see pages 27–33)
- Patterns for the Edwardian man's clothes traced and cut out (see page 110)
- For the trousers, shirt and waistcoat, use the patterns for the Victorian man on page 96

Trousers
- Black cotton

Shirt
- White lawn
- Interlining

Waistcoat
- Cotton or silk with a small print
- Matching polymer clay buttons (see page 58)

Tie
- 2mm (³⁄₃₂in) navy silk ribbon

Jacket
- Slate grey cotton fabric
- Matching polymer clay buttons

Boater
- 5mm (³⁄₁₆in) natural hat straw
  Thin card
- 2mm (³⁄₃₂in) navy silk ribbon

1 Trousers, shirt and waistcoat
The trousers, shirt with collar and cuffs, and waistcoat are all made using the patterns and instructions for the Victorian man on pages 95–7.

2 Tie Use a length of the navy ribbon and tie as shown to make the typical narrow tie of Edwardian times. Tack the ends to the shirt front or tuck them behind the waistcoat.

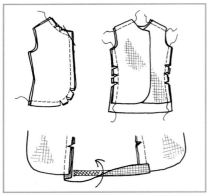

3 Jacket Cut out all the pieces and fray-stop the edges. With right sides together, sew the fronts to the front facings along the front and bottom edges. Clip the corners, turn and press firmly. With right sides together, sew the fronts to the back at the side and shoulder seams. Clip curves and press the shoulder seams open and the side seams towards the back. Use bonding web to press the back hem upwards into place, covering the bottoms of the side seam allowances.

4 Collar Follow the instructions for step 5 of the Victorian man's costume on page 97 to make the collar.

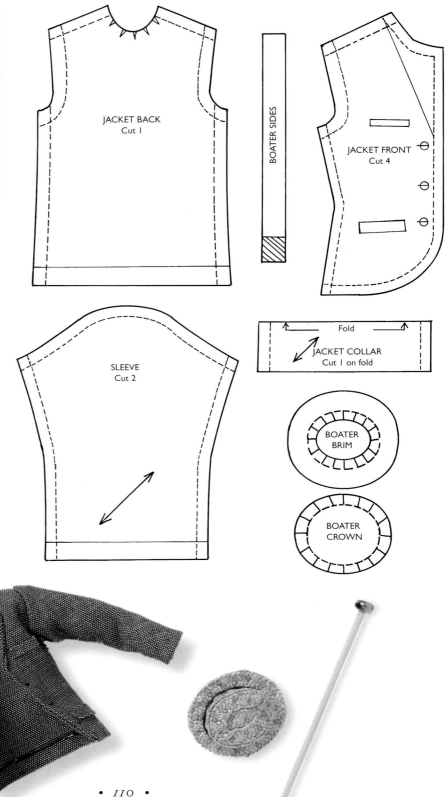

JACKET BACK
Cut 1

BOATER SIDES

JACKET FRONT
Cut 4

SLEEVE
Cut 2

Fold

JACKET COLLAR
Cut 1 on fold

BOATER
BRIM

BOATER
CROWN

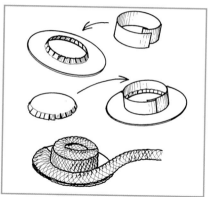

7 Hair Wig the doll in the Edwardian man's hairstyle on page 124. Glue the boater to his head.

Cane The cane is a 10 cm (4in) length of bamboo barbecue skewer with a gold-painted polymer clay ball glued to the top.

5 Sleeves Press up a 5mm (³⁄₁₆in) hem on each cuff using bonding web. Sew the underarm seams and turn. Pull each sleeve on to the doll and ladder stitch to the armhole (see page 64), easing as you stitch and avoiding any puckers.

Finishing Bond together a piece of folded fabric on the cross and cut out the pocket flaps: two wide and one narrow. Glue to the front of the jacket where indicated, the smaller flap on the left breast. Glue buttons to the right jacket front and sew small horizontal stitches on the left front to suggest buttonholes. Glue buttons to the waistcoat.

6 Boater Cut out the boater pattern in card and score along the dashed fold lines. Glue the sides piece into a cylinder, overlapping at the shaded area. Push up the flaps on the brim and glue them inside the bottom of the sides. Push down the flaps on the crown and glue inside the top of the sides. Glue lengths of hat straw on to the hat, easing it round the curves and butting the edges for a neat finish. Use glue to stop the ends fraying. When all the card is covered, glue another strip all round underneath the brim. Glue the ribbon round the crown.

GRANDMOTHER

The grandmother is wearing the Edwardian woman's blouse and skirt in an alternative colour scheme. Her hat is decorated with rosettes and feathers.

Edwardian Girl's Clothes

By Edwardian times, children's clothes had become far less restricting and were loose and practical. Contemporary photographs often show little girls wearing yoked dresses and pinafores like the one on this little doll.

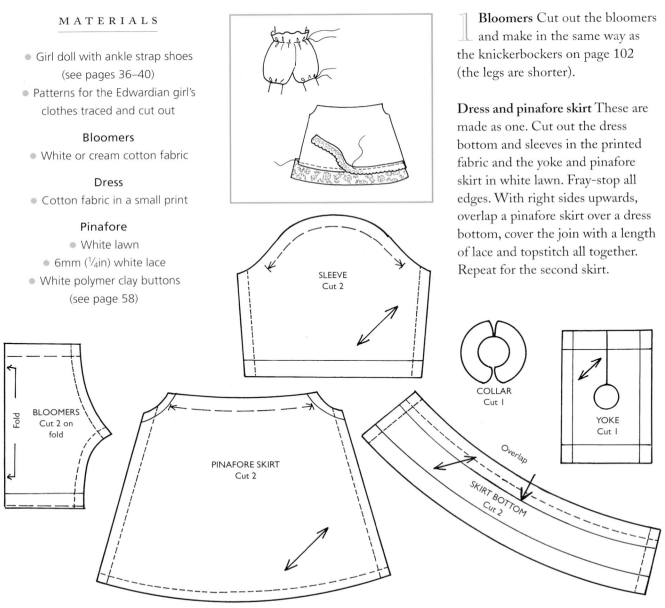

MATERIALS

- Girl doll with ankle strap shoes (see pages 36–40)
- Patterns for the Edwardian girl's clothes traced and cut out

Bloomers
- White or cream cotton fabric

Dress
- Cotton fabric in a small print

Pinafore
- White lawn
- 6mm (¼in) white lace
- White polymer clay buttons (see page 58)

1 Bloomers Cut out the bloomers and make in the same way as the knickerbockers on page 102 (the legs are shorter).

Dress and pinafore skirt These are made as one. Cut out the dress bottom and sleeves in the printed fabric and the yoke and pinafore skirt in white lawn. Fray-stop all edges. With right sides upwards, overlap a pinafore skirt over a dress bottom, cover the join with a length of lace and topstitch all together. Repeat for the second skirt.

SLEEVE
Cut 2

BLOOMERS
Cut 2 on fold

Fold

PINAFORE SKIRT
Cut 2

COLLAR
Cut 1

YOKE
Cut 1

Overlap

SKIRT BOTTOM
Cut 2

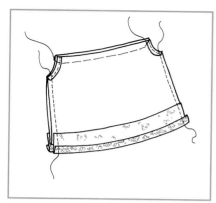

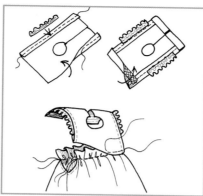

2 **Gathering the dress** Turn under the top corners on each pinafore skirt and stitch or bond in place. Press up the hem on each dress bottom using bonding web. Run a gathering thread along the top of each skirt. With right sides together, sew the skirt front to the back at the side seams. Do not press the seams open as the skirt will hang better.

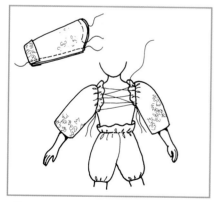

3 **Sleeves** Turn up a hem on each sleeve using bonding web. Run a gathering thread along the top of each sleeve. Sew the underarm seams and turn. Pull up the gathers on the sleeve tops. Pull the sleeves on to the doll and use tacking stitches across the chest and back to hold the sleeves in place.

4 **Yoke** Turn under 3mm ($\frac{1}{8}$in) along each armhole edge and stitch in place. Trim some lace to 3mm ($\frac{1}{8}$in) wide and glue a 15mm ($\frac{5}{8}$in) length under each armhole edge of the yoke. Turn up 5mm ($\frac{3}{16}$in) along the bottom front and back edges using bonding web. Pull up the gathers on the skirt front and back to fit the yoke bottom edges. Lay the yoke front over the gathered front skirt top, covering the raw edges, and top stitch the two together.

5 **Finishing** Put the pinafore on the doll and pull the yoke over her head. Slip stitch the yoke backs in place over the back skirt top edge, covering the raw edges. Slip stitch the two raw edges of the yoke backs together and slip stitch the pinafore loosely to the sleeves under the arms. Glue a thin strip of lace along the bottom edge of the front and back yokes to hide any stitching. Glue a piece of ribbon up the centre back to hide the join.

6 **Collar** Bond together two scraps of printed fabric and cut out the collar. Glue in place around the neck to cover the raw edges.

Buttons and sleeves Glue small white polymer clay buttons up the back of the yoke. Finally run a gathering stitch around each sleeve, 10mm ($\frac{3}{8}$in) from the edge, and draw up to gather. Stitch to secure.

Hair Wig the doll in the Edwardian girl's hairstyle with plaits (braids) (see page 125).

Edwardian Boy's Clothes

The sailor suit was one of the most popular styles for little boys during the second half of the nineteenth century and continued to be worn, with many variations, well into the early twentieth. By this time, the original knickerbockers were often replaced by trousers that reached to just below the knee.

MATERIALS

- Boy doll with boots (see pages 36–40)
- Patterns for the Edwardian boy's clothes traced and cut out

Trousers
- Navy blue cotton fabric

Sailor blouse
- White lawn
- Interlining
- Navy blue cotton fabric
- 2mm (³⁄₃₂in) white soutache braid
- 2mm (³⁄₃₂in) white silk ribbon

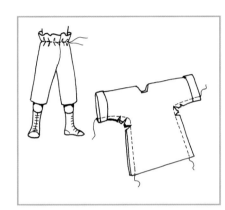

1 Trousers Cut out the trousers and press up the hem using bonding web. Make the trousers as for the knickerbockers on page 102, leaving the leg bottoms ungathered.

Blouse Cut out the blouse in white lawn and fray-stop all the edges. Turn up the hem on the sleeves using bonding web. Fold right sides together and sew the side and under-arm seams. Clip curves and turn.

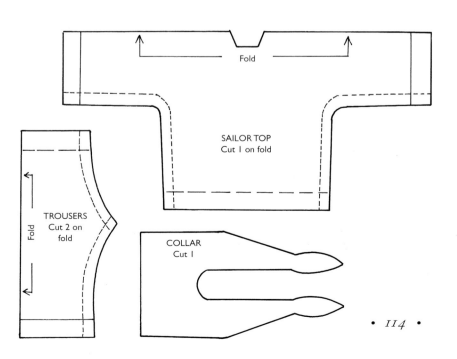

SAILOR TOP
Cut 1 on fold

TROUSERS
Cut 2 on fold

Fold

COLLAR
Cut 1

2 **Gathering the blouse** Make a 10mm (³⁄₈in) cut at the top of the centre back so that the blouse will go over the doll's head and pull on to the doll. Slip stitch the back cut closed, folding one side over the other. Run a gathering stitch around the bottom of the blouse 3mm (¹⁄₈in) from the edge. Pull up to gather and stitch to secure, tucking the raw edge inside and belling the blouse over.

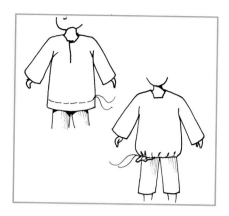

3 **Sailor collar** Glue a piece of white soutache braid across the neck opening, clipping the opening a little wider if necessary. Iron interlining on to a small piece of navy blue fabric and cut out the sailor collar. Glue this in place around the neck, using a dab of glue to hold it down at the back and front and crossing the two fronts over.

4 **Finishing** Glue a line of white soutache braid all round the edge of the collar. Tie the fronts together with white ribbon, finishing with a bow (see page 58). Run a gathering stitch round the bottom of each sleeve and pull up to gather, stitching to secure.

Hair Wig the doll in a short curly boy's hairstyle (see page 125).

EDWARDIAN BABY'S CLOTHES

After the frills of Victorian times, babies were at last dressed more simply, although some contemporary photographs show this to have been a slow process! The baby in the picture is wearing a short baby gown trimmed with lace and a bare head to show off his curls. Use the pattern and instructions for the Tudor baby gown on pages 76–7 and trim the hem with lace.

CHAPTER II

MAKING WIGS

This is often seen as a difficult part of doll-making but if you follow the instructions carefully and methodically you will soon be creating wigs to be proud of. The main secret of making wigs for miniature dolls is to think 'hair' and not 'wig'. This is because the heads are so tiny, you will be gluing hair directly to the head rather than creating a separate wig to fix afterwards. It is best to work directly on to the doll's head as it is easy to remove the hair and start again if you do not like the results. All the curls and partings are put into the hair first, then it is glued to the head, allowed to dry thoroughly and finally trimmed to the correct length if necessary.

Make the wig as the very last stage of your doll after you have finished the clothes. This avoids the hair being spoiled by all the handling while dressing the doll. Wrap the doll's body in clingfilm (plastic wrap) if you are worried about glue from the wig spoiling the clothes, but I find that it is sufficient to prop the doll in a glass or jam jar, arms akimbo, to hold it upright while you work.

MATERIALS FOR THE DOLLS' HAIR

Two different types of dolls' hair have been used for the dolls in this book. Mohair is a natural fibre while viscose is a man-made alternative. Both are available from doll and miniature haberdashery suppliers by mail order and their advertisements can be found in doll's house magazines. All the wig-making techniques in this book can be used on either material but I prefer viscose for tiny dolls as the results are silkier, which looks more in-keeping with the scale.

A good range of hair colours is available in both mohair and viscose; many different shades of brown and fair hair as well as greys and white. Try to choose the more subtle colours and avoid extremes such as bright yellow blond or jet black.

TOOLS

If you do not have all these items at home, they will be readily available in craft shops and stationers.

Curling Tools

- **Metal knitting needles** In various sizes from 3mm ($\frac{1}{8}$in) to 1.5mm ($\frac{1}{16}$in) for ringlets.
- **Thin wire** For very thin ringlets, 0.6mm jewellery wire is ideal.
- **Pipe cleaners** Short lengths for holding the hair on the needles.
- **String** about 2mm ($\frac{3}{32}$in) thick for waving hair.
- **Bulldog clip** For clamping hair.
- **Paper clips** For temporarily holding plaited ends of hair to prevent unravelling.

Cutting Tools

- **Scissors** Use a pair of really sharp, pointed, embroidery scissors.
- **Scalpel or sharp blade** Useful for trimming the upper edge of beards and receding hair.
- **Soft paintbrush** For brushing away stray trimmings.

Other Tools

- **Tweezers** Angled tweezers are best and are useful for applying tiny curls and ringlets.
- **Thread** When making partings, you will need sewing thread in the same colour as the doll's hair. Polyester thread is best as it is finest.
- **PVA glue** This is the best glue to use for making wigs as it dries clear and flexible. If you are unhappy with the results when it has dried, you can peel it off the doll's head along with the hair and start again. My favourite is Aleene's Tacky Glue, which is available from craft shops, but most PVA glues will be suitable.

WIG-MAKING TIPS

- Always try to keep your fingers as clean of glue as possible.
- Apply PVA glue in a thick coating to the doll's head so that it makes a continuous cap. Press the hair on as described in the various instructions. The trick is to make the hair secure by holding the bottom layers in the glue while the top layer remains as dry as possible. If the glue is allowed to come through to the top layer of hair it will show and look unattractive.
- Use very sharp scissors for trimming hair so that they do not drag at the hair and pull it out.
- Apply hair that is too long and trim back afterwards when the glue is dry.
- Once the hair is applied, you will find that you can push it around a good deal before the glue has dried. Use a blunt needle or your finger to do this.

APPLYING LAYERS OF HAIR AND FRINGES (BANGS)

This method of holding sections of hair will help you to have more control, so it is worth practising. It is used for fringes and men's and boys' layered hairstyles.

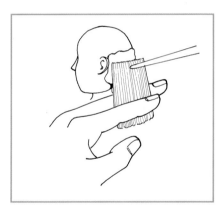

Spread some hair out on your working surface and cut off a section about 15mm ($^5/_8$in) wide and a few centimetres long. Apply glue to the doll's head. Hold the hair spread out between your fingers with about 13mm ($^1/_2$in) protruding. Trim this end straight and press the upper edge of the hair on to the head. Trim roughly to length. Repeat as necessary, always working from bottom to top. Trim when the glue is completely dry.

RINGLETS

These are very easy to make and are useful in a wide range of hairstyles. Use a needle the same thickness that you want the ringlet to be.

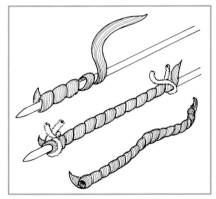

Take a strand of hair, about 3mm ($^1/_8$in) diameter when squeezed together and 15cm ($5^7/_8$in) long. Wind the strand along a metal knitting needle, fixing the first end in place with a twist of pipe cleaner. Wind all the way along to the end, twisting the needle to wind the hair and trapping in further strands of hair as necessary. Keep the hair tight round the needle – each wind should only slightly overlap the one before. When you reach the end of the needle, twist a second piece of pipe cleaner round the end of the hair to hold it in place. Wet the hair, squeeze dry with a towel and place the wound needle in a cool oven at about 100°C/212°F/gas $^1/_4$ for 30 minutes until it is completely dry. Remove the pipe cleaners and slip off the needle.

The same method will work equally well with fine wire for very

thin ringlets. Do not use pipe cleaners but simply bend the ends of the wire over to hold the hair in place.

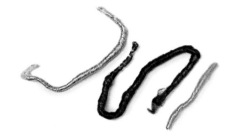

Using Ringlets

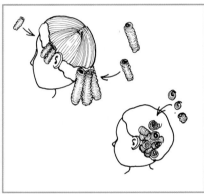

Ringlets are used in many ways; coiled for buns, to frame a face and in the traditional way, hanging all round the head. To attach ringlets, apply a thick layer of glue to the head and also over any cut ends of hair you wish to cover. Cut the ringlet into lengths of about 10mm ($^3/_8$in) long or as required. Press the top of each ringlet's side into the glue and tease out the top hair with the point of a needle so that it merges with any already applied hair and looks as though it is part of it. For shorter styles and baby hair, you can cut the ringlets into very short lengths and glue them end-on to the head.

WAVED HAIR

This method is useful for hair that just requires gentle waves and is particularly good for men's styles.

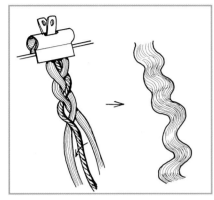

Take a strand of hair about 6mm ($\frac{1}{4}$in) thick and 15cm (6in) long and split it into two. Take a piece of string or twine the same length and, using a bulldog clip or similar, clamp all three lengths together on to a piece of card or a book cover. Now plait (braid) the three lengths tightly together – left over centre, right over centre – to the end. Remove from the book and secure both ends with paper clips. Wet the plait thoroughly and squeeze in a towel to remove excess water. Put in a cool oven at about 100°C/212°F/ gas $\frac{1}{4}$ for 30 minutes as for the ringlets. Unravel the plait and remove the string; the hair will have lovely irregular waves. You can use thicker hair and string for more gentle waves.

PLAITS (BRAIDS)

Plaited hair is very useful for twirling into a bun, for making 'earphones' and for little girls' plaits.

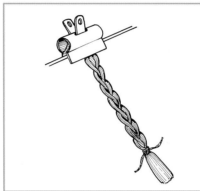

Take a strand of hair about 15 cm (6in) long as thick as you want the final plait to be; I find 3mm ($\frac{1}{8}$in) a good thickness. Clamp one end to a heavy book with a bulldog clip. Split the strand in three and plait – left over centre, right over centre – until the plait is the correct length. For girl's plaits, tie the end tightly with a piece of thread to secure before adding a ribbon bow. Trim about 6mm ($\frac{1}{4}$in) below the tie. If the plait is part of a woman's style, apply a little glue to both ends to prevent it unravelling until you need it.

PARTINGS

These are very easy if you have a sewing machine.

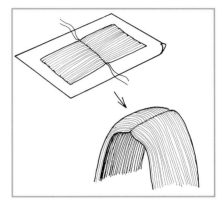

Take a length of hair long enough to go from one side of the head to the other with plenty of extra length. Spread out the hair until it makes a fairly thin layer but you cannot see spaces through it. Take a section wide enough to reach from the hairline at the top of the face round to the middle of the back of the head. Lay this on a piece of paper and sew along the middle of the hair, pushing the hair into the needle to stop it spreading too thinly. Trim the threads and carefully tear away the paper. Before use, turn under 3mm ($\frac{1}{8}$in) at each end of the parting. The parting can be glued centrally to the head or to one side.

If you do not have a sewing machine, sew down the centre of the hair with tiny stitches in backstitch.

WOMEN'S HAIRSTYLES

Women's hairstyles of the periods covered in this book are always upswept or covered with a hat or headdress. Instructions for making the latter are given in the chapters on dressing the dolls. With miniature dolls, it is important to avoid bulk in the hair when giving a doll a hat so it is often better to apply a few curls where they would show rather than giving the doll a complete wig and then gluing a hat on top.

Three methods of creating upswept hair are given here. Each style will then need a bun or ringlets to complete it.

Simple Style

This style gives the effect of hair that is tightly drawn up. The cut ends around the face should be covered with curls or ringlets to soften the effect.

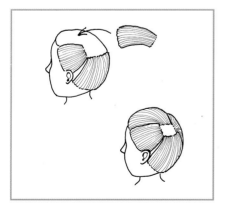

Spread out some hair and choose a length with a slight wave that will curve around the head. Apply a coating of glue all over the head up to the natural hairline. Apply the hair to the head using the fringe technique on page 118, placing the cut edge of each section on the hairline and laying it inwards towards the crown.

Parted Style

This gives a lower backwards sweep to the hair.

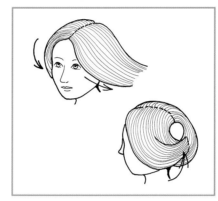

Sew a parting down the centre of a length of hair 10 cm (4in) long and about 25mm (1in) wide (see page 119). Turn the front edge under 3mm ($\frac{1}{8}$in). Apply a coating of glue to the head and press the parting on to the centre of the head. Sweep the front of the hair backwards over the ears and pull one side upwards again, trimming it so that the ends are just below the back end of the parting and held in the glue. Repeat with the other side.

Loose Style

This method gives a fuller, more relaxed result and is a simple way to do upswept Edwardian hair.

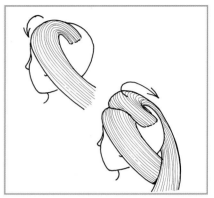

1 Prepare two straight lengths of hair, each about 10mm ($\frac{3}{8}$in) wide and 75mm (3in) long. Apply a coat of glue to the doll's head. Starting at the centre back of the head, press on one end of a strand and curve it upwards, then down the left side of the doll's face, covering the left ear, and round to the nape of the neck. Apply more glue to the top end of the first strand. Now repeat with the second strand, laying it over the first strand, round the other side of the head and curving down.

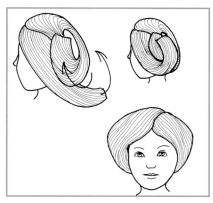

2 Between them the two strands should cover the whole of the head apart from the area at the centre back. While the glue is still wet, push the hair into an attractive shape around the face and leave to dry. Apply glue to the back of the head and press the two ends upwards on to the glue, trimming them off.

Buns

Buns should be glued into place after the glue used for the basic upswept style has dried completely. You can coil the bun loosely or tightly to vary the effect.

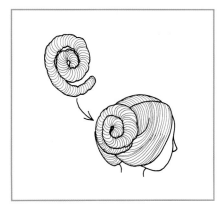

To make a bun, take a 50mm (2in) length of ringlet or plait

(braid) and wind it into a coil. Apply glue to the centre of the back of the head, covering the cut ends of the already applied hair. Press the coil lightly on to the glue, tucking the ends under.

WOMEN'S PERIOD STYLES

Tudor Style

The Tudor hairstyle is a headdress and is described with the costume on page 69.

Regency Style

Cover the head with the simple upswept style and glue thin ringlets round the front and sides of the face, making the ringlets longer at the sides. Glue a coiled ringlet bun to the top of the head.

Victorian Style

Use the parted upswept style and glue on a 10cm (4in) plait coiled into a bun. As an alternative, glue on a fall of ringlets instead of a bun.

Edwardian Style

Cover the head with the loose upswept style and glue on a loosely coiled ringlet or plaited bun.

MEN'S HAIRSTYLES

Men's hair is often the downfall of male dolls as short hairstyles do not have the benefit of copious curls to cover a multitude of sins! This is a pity for they are not difficult and these instructions will show you how to make realistic hairstyles for your men dolls. The cutting techniques described are borrowed from real hairdressing methods.

Basic Hairstyle

This is the basis of all men's short hairstyles. You can use straight or wavy hair.

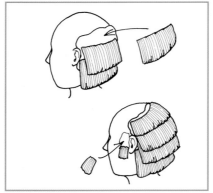

1 Spread out the hair and choose a section about 20mm (³⁄₄in) wide and several centimetres long. Using the fringe method of applying hair on page 118, glue several layers of hair up the back of the doll's head and round the sides, keeping the ears visible and leaving the hair fairly long to be trimmed later. You will need to overlap each layer over the top of the lower layer. Apply glue to the sideburn area and press on small pieces of hair, layering them as before. Leave them long as they will be trimmed when the glue is dry.

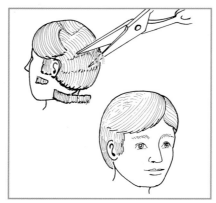

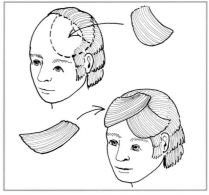

2 Spread glue over the crown of the head, covering all the top ends of the side and back hair. Take a section of hair and curve it round the head and over the cut ends of the applied hair, sweeping it to one side as shown. Take another section and apply in the same way, overlapping the first curve and sweeping down on the other side of the face. Check the crown of the head is covered, applying a little more hair if necessary. Tease the cut ends on top into the hair beneath with the point of a needle. Allow the hair to dry.

3 Trim the back bottom edge along the natural hairline. Hold the scissors almost parallel to the back of the head and snip over the back hair, giving the effect of layered or shingled hair. Trim the sideburns and around the ears.

BEARDS AND SIDEBURNS

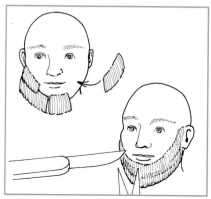

Apply glue to the chin area and press on sections of fringe, trimming the bottom edge roughly. Apply another layer above the first and, if necessary, a third layer. Allow to dry and then trim, angling the scissors to grade the hair. The top edge of the beard can be neatened by cutting along the top line with a scalpel and any hair or glue above the line scraped away. Be careful not to make a cut in the clay where it will be visible. You can make flamboyant Victorian sideburns in this way, applying the lower hair first and layering upwards.

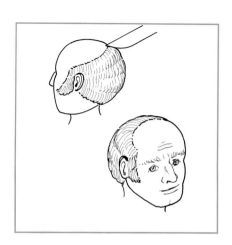

MOUSTACHES

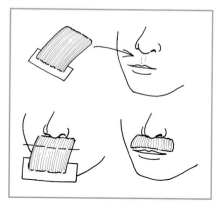

The doll's face is so small that a moustache is a very tiny fringe. It is easier to control the hair if you glue a small section of fringe to a piece of paper first and allow it to dry. Trim the edge of the fringe. Apply glue to the top lip and, holding the fringe by the paper, press the trimmed end on to the top lip. Leave to dry and then lift the fringe by the paper so that you can get your scissors under the hair and trim it neatly to just above the mouth.

RECEDING HAIR

For receding hair or baldness, be sure to sculpt the head with a good round crown that is as smooth as possible. Follow instructions for the back and sides of the man's short hairstyle and leave the crown bare. Trim the top edge with a scalpel as for the beard. You could even glue a few wisps across the crown to suggest hair carefully combed to hide the pate!

MEN'S PERIOD STYLES

Tudor Style

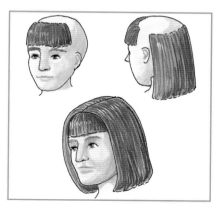

Apply a short fringe to the front of the head and another at shoulder length to the back (see page 118). Glue a section of parted hair (see page 119) over the cut ends and trim to just above shoulder length.

Regency Style

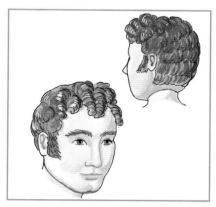

Use waved hair in the basic short style (see page 122) and glue on neat sideburns. Apply ringlet curls (see page 118) to the front of the head, tumbling over the face. Facial hair was rarely worn.

Victorian Style

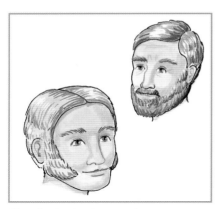

Use the basic short style on page 122. You can add a middle parted section (see page 119) to the top of the head for the typical Victorian look. Flamboyant sideburns and beards are also typical of the period (see page 123).

Edwardian Style

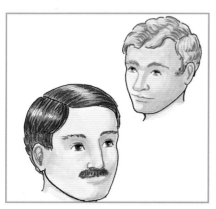

Use the basic short style on page 122. Young men were usually clean shaven and moustaches neatly trimmed while side partings were popular (see page 119).

GIRL'S PERIOD STYLES

Children's hair is fun to do because it is usually less formal than adult styles.

Tudor Style

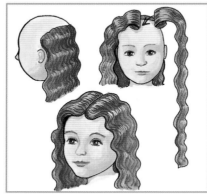

Use long waved hair (see page 119) and glue a fringe to the back of the head (see page 118). Turn under the end of another length and glue down one side of the head, the folded end along the line of a centre parting. It should overlap the back hair. Glue a similar length to the other side butting up to the first length along the parting line. Arrange the hair and trim neatly to length.

Regency Style

Glue waved hair (see page 119) into a short style all over the doll's head, starting at the back and working round the sides. Use the technique of the man's basic style on page 122 for this, leaving the hair longer. Finally glue curls over the crown to hide the ends of the back and side hair and glue several waves across the front to frame the face.

Victorian Style

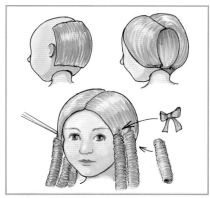

Glue a fringe of straight hair to the back of the head, trimming at the hairline (see page 118). Make a section of straight hair with a parting (see page 119). Glue the parting in the centre of the head and sweep the ends to the back, trimming them at the back hair line. Glue ringlets (see page 118) all round the head at about ear level, covering the hair line. Tease out the top of each ringlet to make it look as thought it is part of the top hair. Glue a tiny bow on each side of the head, just above the ringlets (see page 58).

Edwardian Style

Make two plaits (braids), about 3mm ($^{1}/_{8}$in) thick and 50mm (2in) long (see page 119). Tie the bottom ends with thread. Fan out 10mm ($^{3}/_{8}$in) at the top of each plait and glue this to the doll's head so that the plait itself starts just behind each ear and the fan is spread over the head. Glue waved hair over the back and sides of the head, covering the tops of the plaits. Tuck under any cut edges and keep the ears just exposed. Glue several waves over the crown and front of the head to cover all the other cut ends.

BOY'S PERIOD STYLES

These are nearly always youthful versions of men's hair. For Tudor boys, follow the instructions for Tudor men and cut the hair a little shorter (see page 123). The Regency boy can have the same style as the man with longer curls at the back and omitting the sideburns (see page 123). For Victorian and Edwardian boys, use the men's instructions, again omitting sideburns (see page 124).

BABIES' HAIR

For a curly look, make a fine ringlet (see page 118) and cut it into short lengths. Glue a mass of curls all over the baby's head (see page 118). Babies in bonnets need only have a few curls or a lock of straight hair glued inside the front of the bonnet.

Suppliers and Further Reading

POLYMER CLAY SUPPLIERS

Polymer clays are available in craft and art material shops and also by mail order from craft suppliers. If you have problems finding the clays, the following suppliers should be able to help.

AUSTRALIA

CAM
197 Blackburn Road
Syndal VIC 3149
(Modelene)

Rossdale Pty Ltd
137 Noone Street
Clifton Hills VIC 3068
(Super Sculpey, Premo)

Staedtler (Pacific) Pty Ltd
PO Box 576
1 Inman Road
Dee Why NSW 2099
(Fimo)

CANADA

KJP Crafts
PO Box 5009 Merival Depot
Nepean, Ontario K2C 3H3
(Super Sculpey, Premo)

Staedtler Mars Ltd
6 Mars Road
Etobicoke
Ontario M9V 2K1
(Fimo)

NEW ZEALAND

Golding Handcrafts
PO Box 9022
Wellington
(Du-Kit, Fimo)

New Image Art Supplies Ltd
23 Woodside Road
Mount Eden Auckland
(Super Sculpey, Premo)

UNITED KINGDOM

Edding (UK) Ltd
Merlin Centre, Acrewood Way
St Albans
Hertfordshire AL4 0JY
(Super Sculpey, Premo)

KARS & Co.
PO Box 272
Aylesbury
Buckinghamshire HP18 9YX
(Creall-Therm)

Specialist Crafts
PO Box 247
Leicester LE1 9QS
(Will export Formello world wide)

Staedtler (UK) Ltd
Pontyclun
Mid Glamorgan CF72 8YJ
(Fimo)

UNITED STATES

American Art Clay Co. Inc.
4717 West Sixteenth Street
Indianapolis 46222-2598
(Fimo)

Clay Factory of Escondido
PO Box 460598
Escondido, CA 92046-0598
(Cernit, Super Sculpey, Premo)

POLYMER CLAY ORGANISATIONS

Please send a stamped addressed envelope when enquiring about membership.

The British Polymer Clay Guild
Meadow Rise
Wortham
Diss, Norfolk IP22 1SQ, UK

The National Polymer Clay Guild
Suite 115-345
1350 Beverly Road
McLean VA 22101 USA

WEB SITE

Current information on suppliers can be found on the World Wide Web site:
http://www.heaser.demon.co.uk

BOOKS

Polymer Clay Miniature Sculpting
CARLSON, Maureen. *How to Make Clay Characters*, North Light Books, Cincinnati, Ohio, 1997
(Figurines of great character)
HEASER, Sue. *Making Doll's House Miniatures with Polymer Clay*, Ward Lock, London, 1997

Making and Dressing Miniature Dolls
ATKINSON, Sue. *Making and Dressing Dolls' House Dolls* David and Charles, Newton Abbot, 1992
(Making dolls from porcelain kits and dressing them)
DODGE, Venus, *Dolls' House Needlecrafts*, David and Charles, Newton Abbot, 1995

Period Costume
BOUCHER, Francois. *A History of Costume in the West*, Thames and Hudson, London 1996
(Filled with reproductions of contemporary paintings and drawings of costumes)
EWING, Elizabeth. *History of Children's Costume*, BT Batsford Ltd, London 1977
SIMON SYKES, Christopher. *Country House Camera*, Weidenfeld and Nicholson, London, 1980
(Contemporary photographs from the nineteenth and early twentieth centuries)

MAGAZINES

Doll's house magazines are an excellent source of inspiration and projects. They also contain advertisements for mail order suppliers of materials used in the projects in this book. They are widely available from larger newsagents.

INDEX